C 614 39 03
GATE SECTION ROW SEAT
TERRACE
Super Bowl XXXI
New Orleans
AFC-NFC WORLD CHAMPIONSHIP GAME
SUNDAY, JANUARY 26, 1997 • 5:00 P.M.
LOUISIANA SUPERDOME
NEW ORLEANS
NFL
$275 ALL TAXES INCLUDED
GATES OPEN AT 2:00 P.M.
XXXI

C 614 39 04
GATE SECTION ROW SEAT
TERRACE
Super Bowl XXXI
New Orleans
AFC-NFC WORLD CHAMPIONSHIP GAME
SUNDAY, JANUARY 26, 1997 • 5:00 P.M.
LOUISIANA SUPERDOME
NEW ORLEANS
NFL
$275 ALL TAXES INCLUDED
GATES OPEN AT 2:00 P.M.
XXXI

HOW TO GO TO THE
SUPER BOWL
FOR FREE

AND OTHER SUCCESS SECRETS FROM
THE VICTORY PLAYBOOK

DAVID J. DECKER

FREILING
AGENCY

Published by Freiling Agency, LLC.

P.O. Box 1264
Warrenton, VA 20188

www.FreilingAgency.com

PB ISBN: 978-1-963701-71-5
HB ISBN: 978-1-963701-72-2
E-book ISBN: 978-1-963701-73-9

CONTENTS

Acknowledgments vii

Introduction: Getting Ready for Game Time ix

SECTION 1 – THE SUCCESS JOURNEY

1	How to Go to the Super Bowl for Free	3
2	The Apollo Solution	23
3	The Apollo Solution (Part 2)	41
4	The Reality Face Punch	61
5	The Reality Face Punch (Part 2)	75
6	Rookie Season	95
7	What to Say When You Meet the Mayor	111

SECTION 2 – SUCCESS SECRETS

8	The Secret to Success in Business............................	115
9	What to Say at the Graduation..............................	125
10	The Best Company to Work for in America	145
11	The Worst Investment You'll Ever Make...............	153
12	How Much to Charge	159
13	How to Lose 20 Pounds..	169
14	How to Be Successful..	187

SECTION 3 – A GLIMPSE OF THE FUTURE

15	The Future of Autonomous Vehicles	195
16	The Future of Garbage	205
17	A Reality Face Punch Rescue Plan for Young People	213

SECTION 4 – FLYING HIGH, STAYING GROUNDED

18   In the Red Zone 229

19   Revealing a Mystery 247

20   A World Without Limits 259

Endnotes 269

ACKNOWLEDGMENTS

First and foremost, for Bobbi—thank you for making our house a home and for doing the heavy lifting in raising our kids, which freed me up to pursue wild dreams.

To Jonni and Joel: You are two of the most honorable and decent people I know. I'm so excited to see what the Lord has in store for you in this next stage of life.

Thanks also to Mark Doll and Rustin Schroeder for your creativity and encouragement.

Then there's the tribe of warriors at Decker Properties—you are the secret sauce to our success. It's a privilege to work alongside you.

And finally, to the Freiling team—thank you for helping bring this book to life.

"Things turn out best for the

people who make the best

of the way things turn out."

—John Wooden

INTRODUCTION

GETTING READY FOR GAME TIME

It was the evening before the Super Bowl, and I still didn't have my tickets. I'd been promised tickets. I'd paid for tickets. I was in a hotel lobby with 70 other football fans, expecting to get tickets. But there were no tickets to be had.

Everyone else dissolved into anger and despair. I was determined to get those tickets.

All I had to do—in 18 hours or less—was track down a ticket scalper I'd never met in a city I'd barely ever been to. In the end, not only did I do that, but employing the success principles outlined in this book made it easy. And just for good measure, I turned the tables on Mr. Scalper and got those tickets free.

Game Time

I'm not a celebrity. I don't have my own reality TV show. In other words, my kind of success is entirely replicable by ordinary people like you.

There are plenty of experts who are only successful at giving advice. My success grew out of the real estate business. However, this isn't a book about how to invest in real estate. Real estate was, for me, just a conduit of accomplishment.

The Apollo Solution

Success is a journey. Along the way, there were some things I learned, like the Apollo Solution. The only thing better than success is a success that happens now. With the Apollo Solution, there is no waiting to be invited, credentialed, or approved. Success starts now, with what you have now, the way you are now. Right now.

Yet life is a marathon, and success is a long-term journey. There can't be wasted time on disastrous detours. Embarking upon the correct path the first time is essential, but hard because sometimes it takes a while to know if you're on the right track. Good thing you have the Apollo Solution to help aim the launch.

The Reality Face Punch

Get the right start, and then avoid as many Reality Face Punches as you can. Avoid them all, and you'll have done much better than I. My face bears the wear and tear from a few encounters that didn't go my way. We live in a world of delusion where we are told to "live your truth" or something is "true for you." Feel free to believe in whatever Disneyfied version of truth you like. In the meantime, the actual truth is winding up to deliver a punch in the face. While most people can be counted on to do right most of the time, I'll introduce you to some unsavory Bad Guys. The important lesson is how to sort evil from the merely inept. Learning that helped me survive, and you will too.

Rookie Season

The beginning of a successful journey is like a rookie season. In Rookie Season, I share how I overcame obstacles at the start of my career. From my first days at a big Fortune 500 company to starting my own office, the lessons came fast and furious. Bumbling my way to gaining the nickname The Terminator was one lesson that could have gone better. When I started my own company, I got kicked out of my office space—twice! Yet, I was often the recipient of the kindness of strangers.

Success Secrets

On my journey, I learned some things. Call them Success Secrets. I'll introduce you to The Best Company to Work for in America, The Worst Investment You'll Ever Make, and How Much to Charge. I'll even show you how to lose 20 Pounds in a case study of how small incremental changes lead to long-term success at even life's toughest challenges. The result is goal attainment, spiritual growth, and even victory on the scale.

Predicting the Future

One secret to success that should be obvious is being able to predict the future. I have some predictions to share with you that will put you ahead of the competition. But first, some credentials. Any fool can make predictions. Only the passage of time can sift the wise from the merely loud. In 2006, I published a book called *Cash in on the Coming Real Estate Crash* about 30 months before real estate markets imploded.

Back to those predictions. I'll share The Future of Autonomous vehicles because they are going to change everything. So far, everything I've read about this future is wrong. I'll also share the Future of Garbage because what could be more fun? You'll see the world in a different way.

Making predictions is risky business. With apologies to baseball great Yogi Berra, predictions are hard, particularly about the future. That's why I like to defer to the master predictor, God. God has included many predictions in the Bible made hundreds of years in advance that have already come true. Others we have yet to see. The bottom line is the Bible is a reservoir of wisdom that has stood the test of time. Why not glean advice from the best source available?

You'll find plenty of scripture in this book taken from various Bible translations. In some Christian circles, there is considerable bloodshed over which translation is best. That's unfortunate. I find that they all have something to add, so I trade between them as circumstances warrant, such as better passage comprehension in one translation versus another. Here are the abbreviations for the various translations used:

ESV – English Standard Version
KJV – King James Version
NASB – New American Standard Version
NIV – New International Version

Hearing from God is a good way to get an education. Good news is needed on the education front because a college degree is priced out of reach for more and more people. In Reality Face Punch Rescue Plan for Young People, you'll hear about policy initiatives that could bring prices down. Since sanity from politicians is something that can't be counted on, there are additional strategies for financing an education that an individual can control.

Flying High, Staying Grounded

Absorbing all these strategies will have you flying high in no time. But it's still important to stay grounded. The Bible says, "For what shall it profit a man if he gains the whole world but loses his soul?" Find out just what this means for you in a chapter called In the Red Zone.

There has never been a better time to be alive, never a better chance to thrive. That's why this book closes with A World Without Limits.

Buckle up and let's get going!

"Do you not know that in a race, all the runners run, but only one receives the prize? So run that you may obtain it."   —1 Corinthians 9:24 ESV

SECTION 1

THE SUCCESS JOURNEY

"In the middle of every
difficulty lies opportunity."
—Albert Einstein

1

HOW TO GO TO THE SUPER BOWL FOR FREE

After Moses led the Israelites out of captivity in Egypt, the Jews wandered in the desert for 40 years because of their unbelief. Similarly, Green Bay Packers fans had their faith tested as the team wandered 30 dismal years between winning their last Super Bowl in 1968 and making it back to the championship game in 1997.

Having suffered through this kind of hardship most of my life, I was not going to miss the Packers' return to glory for the first time since I was five years old. I was going to New Orleans for Super Bowl XXXI!

I wish I could say I just called up Paul Tagliabue, the NFL Commissioner at the time, to tell him to set aside a couple of tickets for me at the 50-yard line. But I confess my contact list was not that deep. Instead, I responded to an advertisement in the newspaper promising ticket and travel accommodations and told them, "I'll take two." Remember, this was before the internet when there used to be newspapers and guys named Moses.

I wish I could remember how much the whole thing cost. Perhaps I suppressed the memory. Probably, the pyramids were cheaper. What sticks out in my mind is that it was expensive, particularly the game tickets.

The arrangement included four nights in a hotel, airfare, and two tickets to the game. But there was an odd twist. The Super Bowl tickets were to be picked up at a hotel on Bourbon Street in New Orleans the night before the game. Yet I did not give this oddity a second thought. Again, this was an era before the internet. I had gone to the physical address of a travel agent near my home that had been in business for decades to finalize the arrangements. The agent assured me they had been using this ticket broker for years without any problems.

Although the ticket broker was on the East Coast and I was in the Midwest, I had the opportunity to speak to him on the phone, convincing myself all would be fine. To this day, I cannot remember the man's name, so I call him Super Bowl Charlie. But I will never forget Charlie's distinctive East Coast accent.

Having made my deal with the devil, or in this case, Charlie, my brother and I flew to New Orleans on the Thursday before the game. I passed the time on the plane, reading the newspaper as we waited for takeoff. I clearly remember reading an article quoting then-Wisconsin Attorney General Jim Doyle advising Super Bowl fans not to leave town without their tickets in hand. Apparently, there had been previous instances when football fans were swindled at other championship games. And still, I didn't worry.

We arrived in The Big Easy a few hours later and proceeded for three days to enjoy the cultural carnival that is Super Bowl week. Every Super Bowl is an event, but it's another thing altogether in New Orleans in the French Quarter. Think Mardi Gras meets the Fourth of July. It's how oldsters wind up saying, "I was young and foolish once, and now I am no longer young!" Then came Saturday evening and our appointment to pick up our tickets at the hotel.

Not wanting to take any chances, we arrived early. Yet we were not the first ones there. There were plenty of Packer fans already crowding the lobby in anticipation of receiving their tickets. I soon became engrossed in small talk with other Packer faithful. At first, I didn't notice that the appointed time for the ticket broker to arrive had come and gone. What caught my attention to our plight was the angry voices of the men and the tears of the women. I finally realized that we had been had. Time to start thinking fast.

There were about 70 Packer fans in that room. My first thought was that it would be better if the 70 of us were speaking with one voice. The alternative was three score and ten disorganized people chasing a slippery ticker scalper hundreds of miles away. And it would be best if that one voice we were speaking with was mine. Accordingly, I obtained the paper and a pen from a hotel clerk and began accumulating the names, addresses, and phone numbers of my fellow victims.

I was still engaged in that process when Super Bowl Charlie's henchman strolled into the lobby. For a moment, I thought we were all going to get our tickets. Instead, what we got was a story.

The associate tried to explain that Charlie was in Biloxi, Mississippi, and his car had been towed for parking illegally. Charlie was supposedly busy rescuing his ride from impound and would be joining us within a few hours to make us whole.

The story was good enough to temporarily convince what was becoming an angry mob not to lynch the associate. But several fans had more than a few questions. Couldn't Charlie just rent another car? Why didn't the associate just go get him? And on it went. Someone even wanted to know where Charlie was staying in Biloxi.

No matter what questions were asked, the associate seemed to have reassuring answers. At least until he got to the query about the hotel where Charlie was staying. The associate claimed Charlie was staying at the Biloxi Sheraton.

Fate had dealt that henchman a cruel hand that day. As chance would have it, Brett Favre, the star Packer quarterback more responsible than any other player for the green and gold ascending to the Super Bowl, grew up in Kiln, Mississippi. Brett Favre was and is a colorful guy, and Kiln is a small town. It was a combination sufficient to brew Packer fans out of more than a few good old southern boys.

Kiln, Mississippi, is only about 40 minutes west of Biloxi. Some of those southern Packer faithful were in that Bourbon Street hotel lobby, and there were two things they knew for sure. One was that they did not have the promised Super Bowl tickets they paid dearly for in advance. The other was that there was no Sheraton Hotel in Biloxi.

The associate's story began to unravel. What little civility there was in that mob vanished like the parting of the Red Sea. Then the police showed up like Pharoah and his army.

It turns out the management of the hotel was not anticipating a Packer fan convention in their lobby. They were gracious about playing the role of surprise host at first. Their patience must have worn thin when it looked like they were going to witness a tarring and feathering. That's when they called 911.

The cops wasted no time clearing the lobby. The whole conflagration was moved out on the sidewalk in front of the hotel. New Orleans' finest grabbed the associate and drew him into a discussion, if for no other reason than to preserve his safety. The police confiscated the associate's cell phone and used it to contact Charlie. In short order, the lead officer called us to attention to make his report.

The good news was that Charlie was in New Orleans just like he was supposed to be. His car was fine and in his possession. On a more pessimistic note, he did not have 70 Super Bowl tickets.

Having made their report, the police concluded the discussion by noting there was nothing more they could do. They ordered us to disperse. But before they left, I got one important piece of information—Charlie's cell number. We also knew Charlie's approximate location. It turns out Charlie was at the Sheraton after all, but it was the New Orleans Sheraton.

The Sheraton was also located on Bourbon Street, right across from a Marriott Hotel. The sidewalks in front of either of these hotels had turned into something akin to a Middle Eastern bazaar. Just about anything you could imagine—legal and illegal—was for sale, including Super Bowl tickets.

I quickly made some assumptions and formulated a plan. It is important to note the other 70 Packer fans had made assumptions and plans as well. There is a reason the women were crying, and the men were angry in that hotel lobby. For them, their Super Bowl journey, their Super Bowl dream, had already come to an end. They were mourning the loss. For me, it was just another day at the office. Allow me to introduce the principle of the Anticipation of Negative Outcomes.

The Anticipation of Negative Outcomes

Getting cheated out of a pair of Super Bowl tickets was just another hand grenade in my foxhole, and those are common. I operate under the premise that things are going to go wrong. I call this the Anticipation of Negative Outcomes. I assume that people are going to screw up, trusted associates are going to betray, long-term employees are going to steal, and partnerships are going to sour. And those are the good days.

A person reading these assumptions might misinterpret this as being a little pessimistic. Rather than apply a label, I would say these things are likely to occur because they already have, at least to me. And there is nothing so special about me that they will not occur again. For that matter, there is nothing so special about you that these kinds of things will not happen to you either. And all these calamities are completely capable of taking place without an assist from either you or me. Never mind that we both occasionally add character and flavor to the disaster with a few mistakes of our own, or at least I do.

The Bible talks about this. The rain falls equally on the evil and the good (paraphrased from Matthew 5:45). I don't even know in which group I belong; I just know I'm wet!

I expect things to go wrong. But this is still not a pessimistic point of view. I also expect to prevail in the face of these calamities.

Note the contrast with the other 70 Packer fans who quickly abandoned their Super Bowl aspirations. First, this was no ordinary cross-section of humanity. These were 70 people successful enough and affluent enough to afford to go to a Super Bowl. Second, apparently, these folks expect their lives to run smoothly. There is something so special about them that adversity is a stranger to them. Therefore, difficulties are unexpected, and the response to them is unprepared. Folks that really live this way usually have a title that goes with their name. It's "your majesty."

The rest of us cannot anticipate the exact details of what will go wrong, but we can be mentally prepared and equipped to handle setbacks.

The first step in response is to remain calm. Notice that the other fans at the hotel had already allowed their emotions to rule their thinking. Witness the tears and obvious anger. The question is, how effective were the tears and anger at solving the problem?

The Bible addresses this circumstance directly and provides the following remedy:

Do not be anxious about anything, but in everything by prayer and supplication with thanksgiving let your requests be made known to God. [7] And the peace of God, which surpasses all understanding, will guard your hearts and your minds in Christ Jesus.

—Philippians 4:6-7 ESV

Those tears and anger were not about solving the problem; they were the manifestation of acceptance of defeat and failure.

The second step is to vigorously apply something I call the Apollo Solution. This solution is so involved it gets two chapters of its own. For now, the Apollo Solution is a means to immediate success. Not when you gain the credential, not when you're finally promoted, invited, anointed, or approved. The Apollo Solution is a success plan that starts now, where you are now, as you are now, with what you have now.

The third step is to make sure that you have a firm grasp of the truth. Then, mix in a healthy dose of wisdom. Finally, all this needs to be done within the context of something I call the Goodwill Paradox, to be discussed shortly.

Since the Apollo Solution has its own chapters, we will set that topic aside and turn our focus to gaining a firm grasp of the truth.

Know the Truth

The Bible says, "You will know the truth and the truth shall make you free (John 8:32 ESV)." I will admit that this is a broader interpretation of this verse. As originally given, the verse addressed being free from the bondage of sin. People are tricked into thinking sin holds the promise of freedom. This is not true. Sin leads to servitude, even incarceration. It is not a leap to find that believing in things that are not true leads to bondage and failure.

Knowing the truth should be viewed as a command. A command like this is needed because in the face of adversity, we tend to dissolve into emotion, self-loathing, and finger-pointing. None of these actions is helpful in solving the problem.

We need a success mechanism that will set us free. When adversity strikes, one of the outcomes is anxiousness and anxiety. Suffering from these emotions is like being in a mental prison. Discerning truth is the key to our release.

Often, when trying to solve a problem, I have found myself saying, "We've got to get to a set of facts." Frequently, instead we are presented with a set of opinions. On that Saturday in New Orleans, there were plenty of opinions being expressed about Charlie. But there was an absence of facts, as we shall see.

The Goodwill Paradox

One of the tools for gaining and applying truth and proceeding to wisdom is a success principle called the Goodwill Paradox. One of the dynamics anyone faces in solving a problem or achieving success is human nature. Those around us are either our success partners or the troublemakers. The Goodwill

Paradox is an attempt to understand the complicated nature of the people in our midst—to understand which is which.

The Bible says that we all have the potential to be one of the troublemakers. Here are just a few sample verses:

For all have sinned and come short of the glory of God.
—Romans 3:23 KJV

There is not a just man upon earth that doeth good and sinneth not. —Ecclesiastes 7:20 KJV

All we, like sheep have gone astray....
—Isaiah 53:6 KJV

This list is by no means comprehensive. The short story is people are certainly capable of behaving badly. But this fact also should be weighed against the desire most people have to do right. Hence the Goodwill Paradox.

Bad Guys

There are some who are routinely dishonest. They make their way through the world preying upon those weaker than themselves or anyone they can fool. Call these the Bad Guys, knowing that they can be women, too. One must be forever vigilant against these unsavory characters. But most people, while still capable of appalling corruption, can also be relied upon to do the right thing most of the time.

Even if that person is a ticket scalper.

The Goodwill Paradox certainly applied to my problem with a pair of AWOL Super Bowl tickets. Add to that a firm grasp of the truth, and there was still a good chance for our hero, namely me, to find his way back to ringside for game time.

Here is why I still had hope when 70 other people had given up: 70 other people assumed they had just been fleeced by a Bad Guy. Seventy other people just assumed that Super Bowl Charlie was a dishonest dealer who intended to steal from the get-go. While there are people like that, they are relatively rare. I know there is a Goodwill Paradox.

None of the facts pointed in the direction that we were dealing with a Bad Guy. Super Bowl Charlie had been referred to me by a travel agent who had been in business for years. The agent appeared to have an ongoing, long-term relationship with Charlie. Further, if Charlie intended to steal, why would he have sent an associate to the hotel to tell outlandish stories? Charlie's fables were a desperate bid to buy time.

Wisdom

Finally, through the application of wisdom, I reached a vital conclusion in my search for truth: Charlie had some tickets. The reason Charlie had some tickets is that he thought by stalling for time, he might be able to solve his problem. Charlie was found to be at the one place in New Orleans where it would be most possible to buy a Super Bowl ticket, the Marriott and Sheraton hotels on Bourbon Street. Clearly, Charlie had at least some tickets.

One can walk into a room of 70 people with a smile and a promise if you are a few tickets short. But you cannot walk into that room unless you have at least a majority you can satisfy. Again, my conclusion was that Charlie had at least some tickets, and all I needed was two.

These conclusions flow from the application of wisdom. And while it may seem obvious, it will help bring things into sharper focus by defining wisdom. The best definition I have ever heard is that wisdom is doing the right thing right now.

Wisdom: Doing the Right Thing, Right Now

Hopefully, the foregoing tale is a demonstration of wisdom. Wisdom was absent upon leaving town without tickets in hand. But wisdom rallied before time expired! The solutions presented should seem sound and obvious. The complication, in this example and so often, is that the solutions had to be found *right now*. This was an application of the Apollo Solution, as we'll explore later. There was no time to attend a seminar or form a focus group. What was needed was a plan of action capable of bringing about immediate results. And that plan had to be thought of and then executed in a strange city among tears, anger, and police intervention.

It was time to find out just how wise my plan really was. All I had to do was find a guy I had never met in a city of nearly a half million people, give or take another hundred thousand football fans. But I did have his cell phone number and his approximate location.

Therefore, I went to the Marriott and Sheraton hotels on Bourbon Street. As I said before, there was a booming black market taking place right on the sidewalk in front of these hotels. As far as Super Bowl tickets were concerned, it was definitely a seller's market. There were plenty of buyers but no sellers at all.

Although I didn't think of it at the time, logically enough, ticket prices typically decline right before the game. Charlie was relying on this phenomenon to fulfill his ticket obligations at the last minute. But there was a problem unique to this year. While past Super Bowls often involved at least one team making a repeat appearance, this Super Bowl had two teams from the championship desert. When fans are there for a repeat experience, they may be more inclined to sell if the price is right. But the Packers had not been to a Super Bowl in 30 years. The dry run for their opponent, the New England Patriots, was shorter but still over ten years. Fans from both teams were determined to attend the game and were not selling at any price.

The problem remained: how to find Charlie? Then, I hit upon a solution. I knew Charlie was desperately trying to buy. So I announced to the crowd that I had two Super Bowl tickets to sell, and I was looking for a guy named Charlie! Suddenly, everyone was Charlie. Fortunately, the real Charlie had that distinctive East Coast accent.

In the end, I was able to use Charlie's cell phone number to my advantage, and I arranged a meeting with Charlie at the top of an escalator in the Marriott. There, I met Charlie for the first time. He bore a passing resemblance to actor Gene Wilder. He seemed stressed, like Willie Wonka when Augustus Gloop fell into the river and spoiled all the chocolate.

I had an interesting conversation with Charlie. First, he was rather disappointed to learn I had no tickets to sell. Second, and fortunately, my brother Fred was with me. Fred stands six feet seven inches tall and looks like a linebacker. I am no slouch either at six-foot-three. Between the two of us, we had Charlie outnumbered three to one.

Charlie wanted to know where the seats were he had promised us. I admitted we only arranged for the cheapest seats in the stadium, in the end zone. As we chatted, Charlie pulled an envelope out of the breast pocket of his windbreaker. From the envelope, he extracted what looked to be about six tickets—all he had. Charlie fanned through the tickets like a poker player with a losing hand. "I don't have any end zone seats," Charlie said, "all I have are these two seats on the fifty-yard line. Will that be okay?"

That was definitely okay.

We had obtained the prized tickets at last. I thanked Charlie like he had just given me an entire chocolate factory. Our conversation got cut short when Charlie's cell phone rang. I could hear the other side of the conversation. The caller inquired, "How are you doing, Charlie?"

"Terrible, how do you think I'm doing?" Charlie answered. He walked away and disappeared down the escalator. Then I did the only thing an anxious, adrenaline-soaked real estate jockey could do—I put the tickets in my shoe for safekeeping.

Later that night, I bumped into one of the other fans from the lobby. He volunteered he still did not have a ticket to the game and asked if we had been able to get any tickets. I mumbled something and tried my best to look unhappy.

Twenty-four hours later, the Super Bowl was over. The Packers won. Desmond Howard returned a kickoff 99 yards for a touchdown, at the time a record. Hall of Fame defensive end Reggie White carried the Lombardi trophy overhead for a victory lap around the field. And I got to see it all from the 50-yard line. It was an unforgettable, euphoric experience, worth every penny, and made sweeter by overcoming a detour down Adversity Lane.

Going back to the ordinary routine of daily life was difficult. The old routine seemed dull. I sent the list of names from the hotel lobby to one of the fans on the list and forgot about it. A few days later, a pleasant surprise came in the mail. My credit card statement arrived, and the charges for the Super Bowl tickets had been reversed! Nothing like another welcome home dose of euphoria.

I quickly understood what had happened. Charlie had not delivered most of the tickets as agreed. In an exercise of the Goodwill Paradox, Charlie tried his best to make a bad situation right by reversing the charges for the entire commitment of tickets. Perhaps he forgot or overlooked that I had received my tickets.

I knew what I had to do. I called Charlie to report the error. I volunteered to send in the money as agreed. But before sending any money, I needed to keep in mind the Anticipation of Negative Outcomes.

There was a minor point of clarification. Charlie was doing business as ABC Sports. The charge on my credit card was from

XYZ Entertainment. I did not want to pay one entity only to have the other later demand they were entitled to the money. I explained to Charlie all he had to do was instruct both entities to agree in writing who should be paid. Once there was an agreement, I would send in the payment as instructed. This is where the game went into sudden death overtime.

Representatives from ABC and XYZ contacted me in the ensuing weeks. Both claimed they were entitled to the money and demanded payment. My answer remained the same: unless they both agreed on who was to be paid, there would be no payment. But upon agreement, I would send payment immediately to either entity or split it between the two.

In the end, no such agreement was ever forthcoming. These two entities became embroiled in litigation and were not able to agree on what day of the week it was, let alone who I should pay. I never paid either of them.

Going to the Super Bowl for free was nice. Even more valuable was the confirmation of the success principles that I had not yet put into words but was living by nonetheless. Every experience either results in victory or an education. Somehow, I had pulled off getting both.

A few loose ends remain. Why wasn't I angrier with Charlie? In fact, instead of anger, I expressed gratitude toward Charlie. Gratitude was entirely appropriate. That's another byproduct of the Anticipation of Negative Outcomes and the Goodwill Paradox.

Charlie was just another guy that came up short when it counted. But the Anticipation of Negative Outcomes and the

Goodwill Paradox are not just ideas that only apply to others. How many times have I been Charlie? How many times have I made the wrong decision, hurt someone, and needed forgiveness?

There have been times in my life when I needed a break. It's easier to extend a break to someone else if you first settle in your mind that even good people have bad days. Even those that want to do right sometimes come up short.

I could go on, but Jesus said it best in Mathew 18:21-25 in the Parable of the Unforgiving Servant:

> [21] Then Peter came up and said to him, "Lord, how often will my brother sin against me, and I forgive him? As many as seven times?" [22] Jesus said to him, "I do not say to you seven times, but seventy-seven times.
>
> [23] "Therefore the kingdom of heaven may be compared to a king who wished to settle accounts with his servants.[a] [24] When he began to settle, one was brought to him who owed him ten thousand talents.[b] [25] And since he could not pay, his master ordered him to be sold, with his wife and children and all that he had, and payment to be made. [26] So the servant[c] fell on his knees, imploring him, 'Have patience with me, and I will pay you everything.' [27] And out of pity for him, the master of that servant released him and forgave him the debt. [28] But when that same servant went out, he found one of his fellow servants who owed him a hundred denarii,[d] and seizing him, he began to choke him, saying, 'Pay what you owe.' [29] So his fellow servant fell down and pleaded with him, 'Have patience with me, and I will

pay you.' ³⁰ He refused and went and put him in prison until he should pay the debt. ³¹ When his fellow servants saw what had taken place, they were greatly distressed, and they went and reported to their master all that had taken place. ³² Then his master summoned him and said to him, 'You wicked servant! I forgave you all that debt because you pleaded with me. ³³ And should not you have had mercy on your fellow servant, as I had mercy on you?' ³⁴ And in anger his master delivered him to the jailers,[c] until he should pay all his debt. ³⁵ So also my heavenly Father will do to every one of you, if you do not forgive your brother from your heart."

"Do what you can, with what you have, where you are."

—Theodore Roosevelt

2

THE APOLLO SOLUTION

Houston, we have a problem.

Before becoming a cliché, this statement was first uttered by astronaut Jack Swigert on April 13, 1970. What Swigert said was, "okay, Houston, we've had a problem here."

Swigert was on the Apollo 13 mission to the moon when a routine maintenance procedure resulted in an explosion on the spacecraft. It quickly became apparent that getting to the moon was an impossibility. Instead, what ensued was a fight for survival for three astronauts with the only goal a safe return home.

There was no opportunity to pull into the nearest intergalactic big box hardware store to pick up a few spacecraft repair parts. There was no time to attend a seminar on how to fix a spacecraft. There was no chance to form a focus group on the best way to proceed.

Success had to be crafted from what was on hand, with the skill set already available, right now. There was no room for excuses unless you wanted to be the one making the report to the widows. Part of the solution in April 1970 involved duct taping plastic covers harvested from instruction manuals to vent potentially lethal levels of carbon dioxide. There were multiple manual course corrections as the damaged craft hurdled through space at 25,000 miles per hour. It was unconventional and unplanned, but it worked.

Three astronauts, James Lovell, Jack Swigert, and Fred Haise, Jr. owe their lives to the Apollo Solution.

With the Apollo Solution, success starts now, right now. Success must be crafted from what is already on hand. Success must be achieved by who you are now with the skills you have now.

Success can't wait. Success isn't something that happens when you graduate from college, finally get the promotion or walk out the door in retirement. Success starts now. No waiting to be invited or credentialed. No asking permission. No excuses, no delays. The only thing better than success is a success that happens now.

Success must be cobbled together with what you have now. In my business, the leasing agent is often clamoring for more qualified prospects to rent the apartments. But the number of prospects can't always be controlled. What is within our control is how we handle the traffic that comes through the door. We can't always control the number of prospects. But we can close a higher percentage of the prospects. Then if the traffic gets really lean, it's time to stop being passive. Then it's time to visit local employers to promote the offering to folks in human resources that might be working with transferees.

One of our residents remarked to me, "I rented an apartment from you because I figured that was the only way to get your leasing agent to stop calling me."

Success must be achieved by who you are now. I'm a big believer in education. You can never know enough ever to stop learning. However, inexperience and a lack of knowledge can never be a reason to postpone the success journey.

The first apartment building I ever built, I acted as my own general contractor and construction expeditor. I had no qualifications for doing that and no idea what I was doing. I can remember several occasions when I pulled up to the job site to encounter teams of construction workers with arms folded over their chests upset about another step or circumstance that I had screwed up. I also remember working past midnight and starting again in the morning about 5 AM.

But the result was the Fairways Apartments, an apartment complex on a golf course. That was 25 years ago. I happen to think the Fairways are the nicest apartments in town. But I suppose that's subjective. What is not subjective is that they are the most expensive rentals in town, both then and now.

For that matter, years earlier when I first started buying existing apartments, I had no money or track record. I would put together some ridiculous high leveraged deal on an old beat-up apartment building and then get rejected for financing at every bank in town. But with every rejection I learned something. Ultimately, I kept the deals on course and on time, secured the financing, and became an owner.

The Apollo Solution demands that success starts immediately. Still in school? Start networking now in your chosen field. Do you pine to live somewhere else? Put the for-sale sign in the yard and start packing. Today.

I was 23 when I bought my first apartment building. I was 27 when I started my own real estate company. Things may have gone better had I waited. But sometimes waiting means never getting started. Certainly, had there been foreknowledge of every difficulty I would face, I may have been too intimidated to start. Sometimes being naïve is an advantage. All problems and difficulties cannot be anticipated. Don't postpone your move until circumstances are ideal. They will never be ideal. Jump in now while you still have the resolve.

Don't Quit Your Day Job

When I said don't postpone your move until circumstances are ideal, I was only talking about getting started. Passion is no substitute for cash when the bills show up. Passion means that you're willing to work two jobs until the new gig starts to gain traction. Get started and get going, but don't jump off a cliff.

Define Success

Before we begin, we need to understand where the spacecraft is going. What is success exactly? Only you can define that.

For some, success means restoring a relationship or beginning a new one. Others might be seeking spiritual growth. No doubt some are pining for a big pile of money. This is just the beginning. There are as many definitions of success as there are people.

The first question is, does your idea of success come from you?

Does Your Idea of Success Come from You?

This may seem like an odd question. Of course your idea of success comes from you, where else could it come from?

There are a multitude of influencers whispering about what success is supposed to look like. Let's explore a few.

- **Advertising**

Annual advertising in North America is approaching $300 billion. There's a simple reason all this money is spent on advertising—it works. The advertisers certainly believe they can influence your decisions and they're putting their money where their mouth is.

Advertisers showcase their products or services to inspire envy and action. If you can't afford it now, it's something to aspire to or borrow for!

- **Cultural Expectation**

These influences are wide ranging. They tell us men can't be nurses and women can't be plumbers. It's all the occasions when there is an expectation of what you should or shouldn't be doing yet you can't quite explain why.

Try this on for size. Do you own several pairs of denim pants in blue? How do all these independent thinkers arrive at the same fashion conclusion? While we're here, what about ripped jeans? That purchase decision didn't occur in a vacuum.

It's comfortable to fit in, uncomfortable to stand out. But sometimes success demands veering off the accepted path and blazing an unfamiliar trail.

I had a coveted job with a large Fortune 500 company right out of college. When I left that job to become a commissioned real estate agent selling apartment buildings, many of my colleagues thought I had lost my mind. But had I not taken this gamble, I wouldn't be where I am today.

I Quit My Day Job

By the time I left my first job out of college, I had already owned my first apartment building and had obtained the advice of numerous experts in real estate—some of whom suggested getting started as a broker. I knew I loved real estate, enjoyed pursuing deals and being a landlord. I was single and my expenses were low. In others words, this wasn't the leap off a cliff described earlier, it was more of a hop to a greener pasture where I already knew I would be happier.

Back to discussing those influencers shaping your idea of success.

- **Parents and Family**

Parents certainly should have a vision for the kind of person their child will become. However, sometimes this vision is clouded by vocational aspirations instead of character aspirations. In other words, parents should hope to raise children of strong character. Then leave the children alone to apply that strength of character in pursuit of dreams all their own.

Instead, adult children are sometimes drawn into the family business, like it or not. Or grandpa was a doctor, mom was a doctor and it's expected the next generation will be doctors too.

The way parents shape preferences are too numerous to count. A child's preference for faith, politics, and education is all profoundly impacted by their parents. Spending and saving assumptions are often learned at home. Certainly, the decision to use cigarettes and alcohol or other drugs are influenced by parents.

Then what about sibling rivalry? Some people are doing what they're doing or living the way they're living in the latest round of sibling one upmanship.

- ### Social Media

Social media can be an envy machine. Someone gets dressed up in their best outfit on their best day at their favorite experience. Then they share the pictures of that with the rest of the world like it's just another day.

In fact, what are people called that have a large audience on social media? Influencers.

A 2023 Modern Wealth Survey from Charles Schwab found that social media can introduce doubt about how wealthy people perceive themselves. 47% report feeling wealthy because they can afford a lifestyle comparable to their friends. Put another way, this 47% feels good because they have kept up with the

Joneses. 34% of the users of social media in the survey admitted to making purchases based on what they find friends and influencers buying.

This list is hardly comprehensive. In short, there are plenty of potential influencers trying to tell you what success is supposed to look like. To one degree or another, all of us drink from this well.

The purpose of this exercise is to reconnect with what you truly want. Not what's nice to have, but what you must have to be able to call yourself successful. Anything worth doing is not going to be easy. Instead, count on making sacrifices to achieve your idea of success.

Let me caution you if your idea of success entails accumulating a great deal of money. The next logical question is, what are you going to do with that money when you get it? Maybe it's not stuff that you're after, but the peace of mind that a fat bank account brings. Whatever it is, make sure you understand you.

Further, this is the no judgement zone. If you want to accumulate a bundle of cash so you can buy a big house, fancy cars, and lead an extravagant lifestyle to impress your friends, admit that and get busy.

But I can't help myself but to share an additional piece of advice. The Bible says Solomon was the wisest man that ever lived. He was rich beyond measure, respected and famous. People came from everywhere to hear him speak. He was the powerful head of the Nation of Israel. And he had women, 700 wives and 300 concubines.

Some might say that Solomon had it all. At the end of his life, Solomon took stock of his success and had this report to make: "All is vanity." Solomon is telling us all he achieved was a waste of time:

> ⁴ I made great works. I built houses and planted vineyards for myself. ⁵ I made myself gardens and parks, and planted in them all kinds of fruit trees. ⁶ I made myself pools from which to water the forest of growing trees. ⁷ I bought male and female slaves, and had slaves who were born in my house. I had also great possessions of herds and flocks, more than any who had been before me in Jerusalem. ⁸ I also gathered for myself silver and gold and the treasure of kings and provinces. I got singers, both men and women, and many concubines,^[j] the delight of the sons of man.
>
> ⁹ So I became great and surpassed all who were before me in Jerusalem. Also my wisdom remained with me. ¹⁰ And whatever my eyes desired I did not keep from them. I kept my heart from no pleasure, for my heart found pleasure in all my toil, and this was my reward for all my toil. ¹¹ Then I considered all that my hands had done and the toil I had expended in doing it, and behold, all was vanity and a striving after wind, and there was nothing to be gained under the sun. —Ecclesiastes 2:4-11 ESV

The idea that Solomon was the wisest person that ever lived does more to illustrate the limits of human wisdom. Solomon pursued an idea of success that was ultimately unsatisfying. Don't do that!

Is Your Idea of Success Really Just a Fantasy?

Do you think you know what you want? Put it to the test. For example, some folks would like to move. It's too cold or too hot where they live, too congested, or too dangerous. They'd rather be close to the beach or up in the mountains. They want to be out in the country or back in the city.

If this is your dream, the Apollo Solution demands that you immediately give notice to your landlord or put a for sale sign in the yard. Get your suitcase out, it's moving day.

If your response is, "but Dave, my whole life is here! I can't move now. I can't leave my (adult) kids, the grandkids, my friends, my job...."

Friend, your success dream is just a fantasy.

The same concept applies to your job. Feeling stuck? Frustrated about the path your career has taken? Then do something about that immediately. Enroll in school. Gain new skills. Polish your resume and start working your network for a new gig.

What Do You Really Want?

Only you can decide what you want, what is worth sacrificing for. I'll bet everyone reading this can define a life that's ideal for them. And yet knowing that, many that read this will be working at a job they hate, living in a home they don't love and can't afford and trying to pay back debt on stuff they really didn't want. That's why you need to get what you want and love what you have.

Get What You Want, Love What you Have

This could quite possibly be the dumbest section in this entire book! Of course if you get what you want, you'll love what you have. What could be simpler?

Except the idea is presented exactly backwards. To get what you want, you must love what you have first. This is the Ambition Paradox.

The Ambition Paradox

There is nothing wrong with wanting more or desiring to do better. This is what keeps us waking up early and working hard. But if you cannot find at least some contentment in your present circumstances, then chances are, when you get new and improved stuff or circumstances, you won't be content with that either.

The Bible talks about this. Paul said in Philippians 4:11-12 ESV:

> [11] Not that I am speaking of being in need, for I have learned in whatever situation I am to be content. [12] I know how to be brought low, and I know how to abound. In

any and every circumstance, I have learned the secret of facing plenty and hunger, abundance and need.

Paul says that he has experienced both poverty and riches, and in either, he has learned to be content. This is the ace card of the Ambition Paradox.

Being content is not our natural state. It is learned behavior that must be taught. And there are many agents that work hard at placing contentment out of reach.

We have already discussed some of them. The warhorses of discontent include the following:

1. The Advertising Industry

This industry is banking on the idea that when you are buying something, it will not entirely be your idea. Some of this is OK. If the goal of advertising is to make the public aware of a new product or service that's really great or a big improvement over how things were done in the past, what could be wrong with that?

But advertising will tell us that we need a new car, better clothes or a trip to an exotic locale. If we finally obtain these things and visit those places, then we'll be happy like the models in the commercials. This can work against our contentment.

2. Social Media

We already discussed the best day, best outfit, best experience pics no doubt put through the latest enhancing filters before social media upload. Here are a few uploads that you won't see anytime soon:

- Here's my spouse and me fighting!
- Just got up and really hung over!
- Just fell down the stairs!
- Hit a telephone pole with the car!

Social media can be a great way to keep in touch with family, friends and colleagues, but it can also encroach on your peace and contentment.

3. Comparisons

Comparisons prove why social media can be so toxic. Social media is a comparison enabler. Compare yourself to others and you will always be able to find someone who is richer, better looking, more athletic, more spiritual or (seemingly) happier. In fact, insert seemingly before all those descriptors.

An internet search of Bible verses regarding comparing ourselves to others produces over 100 references to choose from. The volume of material alone instructs about the magnitude of this problem. Here are a few of the Comparison 100:

[12] Not that we dare to classify or compare ourselves with some of those who are commending themselves. But when they measure themselves by one another and compare themselves with one another, they are without understanding.   —2 Corinthians 10:12 ESV

[3] Do nothing from selfishness or empty conceit, but with humility consider one another as more important than yourselves.   —Philippians 2:3 NASB

Embracing the idea that everyone you meet has worth, merit and expertise is liberating. You cannot possibly be the best at everything. Accepting this truth takes the pressure off and makes enjoying others more likely.

"Judge not, that you be not judged.

—Matthew 7:1 ESV

In order to judge, you must first compare. We don't know what place someone started from. We don't know what their life is really like behind closed doors.

[17] "You shall not covet your neighbor's house; you shall not covet your neighbor's wife, or his male servant, or his female servant, or his ox, or his donkey, or anything that is your neighbor's."   —Exodus 20:17 ESV

To ignore this commandment is to get caught up in keeping up with the Joneses.

I praise you, for I am fearfully and wonderfully made. Wonderful are your works; my soul knows it very well.

—Psalm 139:14 ESV

God created you in his image. He makes no mistakes!

4. Blaming Others

When others are blamed for the mess we're in, the opportunity to learn from the experience is lost. Additionally, the blamer is not in control, but the victim of circumstance.

We live in a culture where sometimes victimhood is something aspired to. The "victim" is not accountable because circumstances are beyond their control. There is always an excuse. No solution ever proposed can ever work—a sense of powerlessness results, leading to diminished self-confidence. Frustration and anger can sink in, along with resentment of others who seem happy and successful.

Again, the Bible verses addressing this troublesome problem run rampant:

The way of a fool is right in his own eyes, but a wise man listens to advice.   —Proverbs 12:15 ESV

This next verse in Matthew 7:3-5 ESV is one of my favorites and speaks not only to blame, but also to our propensity to make comparisons:

³ Why do you see the speck that is in your brother's eye, but do not notice the log that is in your own eye? ⁴ Or how can you say to your brother, 'Let me take the speck out of your eye,' when there is the log in your own eye? ⁵ You hypocrite, first take the log out of your own eye, and then you will see clearly to take the speck out of your brother's eye.

Romans 2:1
Therefore you have no excuse, O man, every one of you who judges. For in passing judgment on another you condemn yourself, because you, the judge, practice the very same things.

5. Regret

Regret is living in a past that cannot be changed. We are to learn from our mistakes, not wallow in them. Here is a powerful verse from 2 Corinthians 7:10 ESV:

For godly grief produces a repentance that leads to salvation without regret, whereas worldly grief produces death.

This verse tells us that our mistakes should help us recognize our need for a Savior to save us from wrongdoing and consequence. In this way, there is a positive outcome from our mistakes. In contrast, wallowing in our mistakes saps our energy, confidence, and creativity at best and leads to ruin at worst.

6. Worry

Worry is attempting to live in a future we cannot control. Entire books have been written on this topic including the Dale Carnegie classic *How to Stop Worrying and Start Living*. There's no shortage of Bible verses on this topic either.

Do not be anxious about anything, but in everything by prayer and supplication with thanksgiving let your requests be made known to God. [7] And the peace of God, which surpasses all understanding, will guard your hearts and your minds in Christ Jesus.

—Philippians 4:6-7 ESV

…casting all your anxieties on him, because he cares for you. —1 Peter 5:7 ESV

"Therefore do not be anxious about tomorrow, for tomorrow will be anxious for itself. Sufficient for the day is its own trouble. —Matthew 6:34 ESV

Worry is a common affliction and I have not been immune. I'll admit to occasionally suffering from a general sense of anxiety. When this happens to me, I apply Philippians 4:6-7, and first pray and ask God to take these worries from me. Often, that is enough. But if not, then I make a list of all the things that could be the source of my unease. Then I write out what needs to be done to overcome these problems. Even when the resulting tasks are not something that can be executed quickly, this exercise nearly always leaves me restored.

We've considered six warhorses of discontent. In the next chapter, let's consider three ways to cultivate contentment.

And I am sure of this, that he who began a good work in you will bring it to completion at the day of Jesus Christ.   —Philippians 1:6 ESV

"The happiest people do not

necessarily have the best of

everything. They simply make

the best of everything

they have."

—Warren Buffett

3

THE APOLLO SOLUTION (PART 2)

In Part I of the Apollo Solution, we had just finished up riding the six warhorses of discontent. Now let's begin with Three Ways to Cultivate Contentment.

Three Ways to Cultivate Contentment

1. Gratitude

It is said that gratitude is the most fleeting of human emotions. Often, a lack of gratitude coincides with losing sight of the big picture. If you live in the United States of America, you reside in a land of freedom and opportunity unlike anything history has ever seen. You can look forward to a long, productive life span that is without precedent. And yet if you are displeased with the state of affairs, you can have a vote in changing them and vocalize your displeasure without fear of reprisal.

Some reading this accounting will think it naïve. They will cite cancel culture, racism and more. Yet, people the world over continue to risk their lives to come here, fleeing conditions elsewhere that are even worse. Our country is not perfect. But

I'm highly confident the future is bright and tomorrow will be even better.

Tell someone you appreciate them. I'm a landlord renting apartments. Our success or failure hinges upon things like how well we vacuum the halls, pull the weeds, pick up the cigarette butts and other litter and remove the pet waste. Often the individuals tasked with this work are invisible and underappreciated. I try to share with them how important what they're doing really is. And how much I appreciate them for doing it.

There are everyday occurrences that we take for granted, which are unimaginable for people from another time or place, like jet travel and commuting to work in a comfortable, safe, reliable automobile. For that matter, having work that is not backbreaking and life-shortening. We have access to a world of information from a device that fits in a pocket. We take a few pills or get an injection to avoid illness that used to routinely kill millions.

If the input is gratitude, the output is patience and happiness. The logic behind this should be obvious.

2. Acceptance

Accept people and things for who they are, not for how you wish them to be.

Sometimes I have to keep learning this one. I've often said, I'm not in the training business, I'm in the consequences business. Certainly, we need to train new teammates in the nuances of their job so they can be effective. But character is something that we cannot train. That was mom's job. If you show up at

Decker Properties lacking in character, I have yet to find a way to consistently fix that.

Recently, we had a promising young woman join our property management team. She was hardworking, knowledgeable, experienced, and creative. I thought this was someone that could take us places. However, she had a penchant for mistreating subordinates. She was polite and professional with anyone she perceived to be a superior or an equal; however, with someone seemingly in a lesser position, it was another matter. I just shared how we rise or fall on the shoulders of those tasked with the humblest responsibilities. Mistreating these heroes grieves my soul.

I tried to point out to Dawn (not her real name) that this was a conscious choice she was making. One example involved our second-in-command. He came up through the maintenance track. Even now, he can be found visiting apartment buildings in a flannel shirt and work boots. He looks right at home with a set of tools in his hands. When Dawn first met him, not knowing who he was, she treated him as just the maintenance man.

No one at Decker Properties is treated like they're only the _____. I may be stuck on repeat, but to the rest of us that are still thinking, we know we rise or fall based on the state of the hallways, the weeds and the litter. While these tasks may be low skilled and unglamorous, they are vital. Those responsible for these tasks must be treated accordingly. That someone would belittle a teammate that already has what would otherwise be a thankless job is infuriating. It completely goes against our culture.

I tried repeatedly to explain this to Dawn, but the lesson never took. It was a frustrating experience. Dawn was, and is, bright, creative, and hardworking, and I wish her well. She has since left us and if she cannot change the way she treats her team, that is for the best.

The need to accept people and things for what they are, rather than how you wish them to be is certainly not limited to employees. Sometimes, parents, grandparents, siblings, or old friends don't have it in them to be the supportive, loving, encouraging people they are supposed to be. You can continue to beat your head against a wall of frustration expecting somehow these folks will change or behave differently. Or you can accept them for who they are and adapt accordingly.

Accepting people and circumstances for how they are is energizing. Now the positives that remain in these relationships can be enjoyed unfettered by expectations that will never be met.

3. Experiences versus Material Possessions

The junk yard is full of cars that were new once. They may have been someone's pride and joy. Today they are just junk. That's what happens to stuff. Material possessions must be maintained. They must be secured. They are a responsibility.

People quickly adapt to their surroundings. What was once new and special quickly becomes the new normal. Too much stuff is its own burden, called clutter.

But an additional joyful experience never adds to clutter. Our memory of experiences can grow fonder with time, while material possessions deteriorate with time.

We connect with others and form relationships through experiences. I have lifelong friends I met in college and while playing softball.

Experiences make comparisons more difficult. Some people love to hunt and fish. Others would rather travel abroad. How is one better than the other? It depends on who you are.

Let's return for a moment to our earlier question in the previous chapter of what do you really want? Sometimes, our lack of understanding of what we really wanted sends us off course.

How Did We Get Here?

If you see yourself described in What do You Really Want, then understand that you may have fallen under the spell of influencers that have clouded your vision of success. You are like a spaceship that has gone off course. Let's dig a little deeper in the saga of It's Not Such a Wonderful Life:

It's Not Such a Wonderful Life

You didn't really know what you wanted to do, but mom and dad and your friends all expected you to go to college, so you did. You changed majors a few times. It took five years, and the student loans were enormous, but graduation day finally arrived.

Those student loans dictated a well-paying job even though you weren't so sure this is what you wanted for the rest of your life.

Then you met someone! The wedding cost a fortune, but what are credit cards for?

Rather than paying down the student debt and the credit cards, you decided to get into a house—because a house is a good investment, right? Of course, houses are incredibly expensive these days. The one purchased was further away from work than ideal and hardly a dream house, but it's all that could barely be afforded.

Given the commute time, a new ride was in order. It's amazing what you can get for a few extra bucks. The finance company was willing to extend the car loan to 96 months, so the monthly payment changed only slightly.

Then great news, you're going to be parents! It's incredible what day care costs today, but losing an income for one parent to stay home was out of the question. In fact, things were going so well at work that you got a big promotion. Or at least the company thought it was a promotion. It turned out to be a ton of added stress. However, your family needed the extra money, so you took one for the team and accepted the new job.

Then mom passed away. Things had been so hectic, it had been a couple of years since you got back home. Of course, mom and dad had visited many times. But before mom passed away, the visits had been waning. While home for the funeral, it became apparent why they hadn't been visiting as often. They just couldn't get around like they used to. They clearly weren't keeping up the old home anymore. That's when you realized that dad shouldn't live alone.

Dad moved in with you. You helped settle their financial affairs. They had one of those reverse mortgages on their house, so after the funeral expenses, there wasn't any money left.

The kids were getting bigger and needed their own rooms, and with Dad moving in, you needed a bigger place. The new house was even further out, but your boss allowed you to work from home one day per week. The total commute time remained about the same, but those four remaining commute days were a crusher.

Time passed, the kids grew older and dad passed away. Dad didn't have anything left to pay for the funeral. Good thing the funeral home had a finance plan.

It was time to start thinking about college for the kids. Hard to believe they were ready to leave the nest. Harder still to believe that a few of your student loans still required payments!

Life seemed to be like an ever faster moving treadmill, but somehow you were holding it all together. Then came the cancer diagnosis.

It was an emotional time. Family and friends rallied around. Neighbors you hardly knew brought over meals. The surgery was a success, but the chemo and radiation were exhausting. Your employer was incredibly gracious and supportive.

"Take all the time you need and get back on your feet. Your job will still be here when you're better."

Then the medical bills began to roll in. It's amazing what insurance didn't cover. Better or not, you decided it was time to get back to work and get that income coming back in.

Having cancer made you realize that life isn't forever. Going back to all the pressure and the commute after skipping that for weeks brought the realization of just how miserable your pre-cancer life really was.

The one shining light in your life was the adult Bible study class you taught once per week. It made you realize you probably would have been much happier being a teacher. Of course, the pay would have been about a third of what you're making and going back to school or changing careers now is out of the question.

Instead of investigating new career options, you began seeking a referral for someone to help with your depression.

If There Ever Was a Life in Need of an Apollo Solution, It's This One

The proceeding account is entirely fictional, but to what degree does it sound familiar? Note that it's hardly a worst-case scenario. What if divorce had intruded on this saga?

Two recurring themes define this story. A failure to plan and too much debt. It might be the American way, but it's not the American dream.

Before we begin applying an Apollo Solution, we still need to dig deeper into how this spacecraft got so far off course.

Be Careful What You Own and What Owns You

"Be careful what you own and what owns you." My father said this to me when I was young and I have never forgotten. His lesson was centered on loving your stuff too much. But there's more to it than that.

What do you really own? If you owe against it, you don't own it. Consider Proverbs 22:78 NASB: The rich rules over the poor, and the borrower becomes the lender's slave.

Ouch. Finding out your loose financial lifestyle has made you a slave is like a Reality Face Punch (see Chapter Four).

If you have a mortgage, you're not a homeowner, you're a house slave. Renting an apartment? You're a slave to the landlord. Yes, you must live somewhere. How does your home fit into your financial objectives?

If you lease your car or owe against it, you're a car slave.

Carrying a balance on your credit cards? You're a slave to the finance company.

Student loans? It would be nice to say that you're a knowledge slave. It may be acceptable to be a slave to acquiring knowledge, but the acquisition of knowledge was in the past. The debt is still here. You're a slave, call it whatever kind you will.

Being a slave means that your career choices will be limited to those that can service your debt. In this way, the rich are certainly ruling over the poor. Rich lenders get to dictate the kind of job you will have.

Rich people work at jobs they like and do what they want, when they want. But here we risk falling into the trap of believing that being rich equates to having a bunch of money.

The Rich Person Fallacy

Any situation that you can craft where you're working at a job you love, doing what you want, when you want, means you're rich regardless of the balance in your bank account.

Being a contributor and provider gives life meaning, purpose and direction.

Finding a job you love doing is common advice. But it doesn't go far enough. Every job has days that are just a slog. What will keep you going when the joy is on temporary hiatus?

Having a job you enjoy is not enough. You need a cause.

In 2009, I bought a small apartment complex I'll call River Glen Apartments. The property was originally built in 1965. The location wasn't the best. The building had been well maintained but not updated. Probably the best thing about the whole deal was not the building but the managers I inherited, Don and Eileen.

Although retired now, Don and Eileen were, and are, salt-of-the-earth, hardworking people who care. When I first met them, I shared my vision for the River Glen Apartments. I acknowledged that there was some incurable obsolescence. I admitted the location presented challenges. But I also outlined the litany of improvements I planned on making to apartment interiors, heating equipment, landscaping and more. In short, I wound up making an impromptu impassioned speech that crescendoed with this challenge: We were going to make a stand at River Glen. Understanding the limitations that we could not change, we were going to do the very best with what we could change. Whatever limitations existed cannot be an excuse for anything less than producing excellence for everything else within our control.

This was the first time I realized that what I was doing was more than just a job I enjoyed. It was a cause.

I have both built apartments from the ground up and renovated tired buildings in desperate need of attention. While both are rewarding, sometimes it is more satisfying to remake the blighted property into a glamorous gem again.

I feel like I'm making a difference not only in the community where our properties are located, but also in the lives of our teammates that do such a wonderful job running these properties. I know my life is richer for having worked alongside them.

Understanding the need to produce, provide and contribute explains why some people that have a lot of money are still miserable. If they are wealthy through inheritance and not engaged in a productive cause, this can often lead to a life devoid of meaning.

There is even special terminology to define the phenomenon. Affluenza is a term coined to describe the malaise associated with the young and affluent, but it also aptly describes older, privileged folks too.

Avaricious means a person concerned about gaining wealth. It's an unflattering term and conveys the idea that despite wealth already accumulated, the avaricious person is still not satisfied and is clamoring for more.

Then we have vulgarian, a person whose vulgarity is amplified by wealth.

Ultimately, understanding the dynamics of having a cause explains why wealthy individuals continue to work. Simply put, they're not done yet. The cause still merits attention.

People envy others with wealth because they assume that if they could acquire the same wealth, they could quit their miserable jobs. However, wealth is not the panacea it seems. In a recent survey, 35% of millionaires expressed concern about having insufficient funds for retirement.

The same survey indicated 58% of high-net-worth individuals were planning on working longer and 36% reflected that retirement may not be an option.[1]

Put another way, if we cloaked these individuals' net worth and inquired, "Would you want to join a demographic truncheon where 58% of respondents report having to work longer than planned and 36% think retirement is not an option," most people would say no. No, I don't want to be … a millionaire!

I count myself rich not because of the size of my bank account. I have a cause that keeps me getting up early and working hard. Yet I get to do what I want, when I want, which includes things like writing this book. If making more money is the goal, then I should focus my time on further investment in real estate. Writing is for paupers, there is far more money in real estate! But writing this book and joining you on this journey is a blast.

This leads us to busting the retirement illusion.

Busting the Retirement Illusion

The idea of retirement is a recent phenomenon. The idea of accumulating a nest egg to fund a couple decades of idleness at the end of life has only happened in the last 80 years or so. Previously, most people worked until they died. If something happened to you in old age to prevent you from working, poverty was often the result.

Further, the kind of work people did often involved brute force manual labor. Until recently, most people worked at subsistence farming. My father grew up on a farm plowing fields behind a horse.

Today, workers enjoy a carnival of choices and more work opportunities exist than ever before. The problem isn't about having enough saved for retirement. The problem is being stuck in a job you hate. Find a cause worth living for and never give up.

We're just getting started. One positive unintended outcome of disastrous Covid lock downs has been an explosion of new businesses. Forced out of their day jobs, many workers turned entrepreneur.

Bring on the Internet

Pause for a moment to consider the most important invention of all time. Some may dispute it, but I believe the invention of the printing press is the GOAT, the greatest of all time.

Before the printing press, there was no point to educating the masses to, for example, read. Books were handmade, rare and expensive. The printing press changed all that.

For the first time, recording, sharing and disseminating information was made cheap and easy. Technology had the opportunity to build on itself.

For instance, the invention of the printing press led directly to the eradication of cholera.

As printed material became more commonplace, people began to notice that older folks like me had difficulty reading small type. Necessity gave rise to optics. However, those lenses could do more than just help the elderly see better. At a higher power, you could see what was previously invisible, like the bacteria that causes cholera.

The technological explosion in the wake of the invention of the printing press is called the Scientific Revolution.

Now we have the printing press made all over again in the form of the internet. Now the dissemination of knowledge isn't cheap, it's free. And instant.

What does this mean to the Apollo Solution? Simply this— more solutions immediately at hand, the very life blood of the Apollo Solution.

Hate your job? Maybe it's time for you to go into business for yourself. Today, even the tiniest market segment can be reached worldwide through the internet. This makes it possible for the most obscure propositions to find a market.

Years ago, I read an article about the lack of commitment of today's entrepreneurs. In the past, starting a business required a commitment to a brick-and-mortar location and probably quitting your day job. Entrepreneurs had to be, "all in."

How idiotic.

Today, thanks to the internet, anyone with a website can find customers and transact business. More ideas than ever before can make it to market without placing the entrepreneur at enormous risk. You can dip your toe in the pond of business startup without risking your entire financial life. This is a boon to fresh ideas, not a bust.

If you hate your job and starting your own business is not your thing, at least you can search for new jobs on the internet.

Maybe it's your commute that makes you hate your job. Maybe that commute can be eliminated by cutting a deal with your existing employer to allow you to work from home over the internet.

Working from anywhere also puts you sooner on the way to moving to paradise. Not when you retire, now.

Does working remotely also allow you a flexible schedule? Can you compress your 40-hour week into four days instead of five? Then every weekend is a three-day road trip weekend for the travel lover. Or just a little more time off harvested from what might have otherwise been commute time.

The internet is a powerful tool in the Apollo Solution toolbox.

But even before the internet, there were plenty of examples of the Apollo Solution in action. Being a good Wisconsin boy, I can't resist sharing an iteration of Apollo Solution that we'll call the Lombardi Solution.

The Lombardi Solution

Steal industrialist and philanthropist Andrew Carnegie died on August 11, 1919. The same day, out of the ashes of the First World War, the Weimar Republic of Germany was born. And in Green Bay Wisconsin, shipping clerk Curly Lambeau approached Indian Packing Company Owner Frank Peck for $500 for uniforms and equipment to field a new football team, what would become known as the Green Bay Packers.

In those early days, the Packers played in Hagemeister Park in Green Bay on an open field with no fence or bleachers. Boosters would pass a hat to collect donations to keep the team solvent.

The Packers joined the precursor to the NFL in 1921. It would be 1933 before the Packers would have a losing season and by then, the Packers had won three consecutive NFL Championships in 1929-1931. Green Bay returned to dominance in 1934, and won three more NFL Championships in 1936, 1939 and 1944.

1948 brought a season of change. For the next 11 seasons, Green Bay would stumble to a losing season every year, eventually becoming an embarrassment. The 1958 season ended with a record of one win, ten losses and a tie.

Then, as now, registering such a miserable record is apt to result in losing your coaching assignment. Such was the case for the Packers. Filling the vacancy wasn't easy. Several candidates were considered and some were offered the job but declined. Finally, the Packers went with a virtual unknown—Vince Lombardi. What proceeded from there is a matter of history.

For the next nine seasons, Lombardi would post a winning record every year. He was named Coach of the Year his first season. The Packers were winners in 75% of their games and won five NFL championships including the first two Super Bowls.

The record of accomplishment is so great that the trophy awarded to the winning Super Bowl team is called the Lombardi Trophy.

Yet all this accomplishment overlooks one important detail. Lombardi managed to win with largely the same roster he inherited in 1958, the worst season in Packer history. Of the 22 players who started in 1959, 16 were veteran starters from the pre-Lombardi 1958 season, which was the worst on record. Lombardi not only won, he won with the resources he already had. This is the essence of the Apollo Solution.

The Apollo Solution demands that you define joy and success and then immediately remove the barriers to achieving them.

When I was trying to get to the Super Bowl and I found out the night before the game that my ticket wasn't going to be delivered as planned, that was like an explosion on my spacecraft. There were 70 others in the same predicament and their reaction was typical and ineffective. First, there was anger, then sorrow from accepting failure and defeat.

The overriding theme of the Apollo 13 mission post explosion is calm. Those astronauts knew their mission was dangerous. Just three years earlier on January 27, 1967, three astronauts died in a flash fire during a launch rehearsal.

Yet in the wake of the explosion, Jack Swigert alerts his colleagues with, "okay, Houston, we've had a problem here." It sounds like the kind of thing you would say if you spilled some Tang[2] in your lap.

These astronauts were trained professionals. They knew that as long as they were alive, there was still opportunity to solve the problem. Anger and despair have no place in the Apollo Solution. In fact, the Apollo Solution is the remedy to anger and despair.

There are no problems, only opportunities. Solutions are always within our grasp. Sometimes they may seem hidden or unconventional.

The Apollo Solution demands that success start now, the way you are now. Don't ask permission. Don't wait to be credentialed, invited or recommended. Just go.

> But godliness with contentment is great gain, for we brought nothing into the world, and we cannot take anything out of the world. —1 Timothy 6:6-7 ESV

"Everyone has a plan until

they get punched

in the mouth."

—Mike Tyson

4

THE REALITY FACE PUNCH

When you're on your way to the Super Bowl and calamity comes, discerning the truth is an imperative. The Reality Face Punch is the consequence of accepting falsehoods or failing to mine the truth from a shaft of confusion.

We live in a world of delusion where we are told to, "live your truth" or something is, "true for you." Feel free to believe in whatever Disneyfied version of truth you like. In the meantime, the actual truth is winding up to deliver a punch in the face.

Sometimes the Reality Face Punch is literal. Occasionally, in the euphoria of fresh romance, one fails to discern that Romeo is really a thug. A mishappend nose results.

Nothing helps sharpen the mind like a crisp punch in the face. The unfortunate truth is that every entrepreneurial warrior is likely to experience the occasional Reality Face Punch no matter what care is taken. This is where the exceptions to the Goodwill Paradox are found. The Goodwill Paradox assumes that most people can be counted on to do the right thing most of the time. The operational words are most people and most of the time. That leaves room for Bad Guys—remember some are women—to land a fist right where it counts.

We warned about Bad Guys earlier. Some present themselves as trustworthy when they are not. I have met a few of these unsavory characters through the years.

A Stinging Betrayal

Years ago, I was in the midst of exiting a real estate partnership. Tragically, all friendly means of dissolution had failed and litigation ensued. There was no end to quarreling over minor property management issues. This quarreling was a distraction to resolving the larger matter of how to divide a few hundred apartment units. I felt that temporarily placing the apartments with an outside management firm would alleviate the management issues and help us focus on dissolution.

To that end, I thought my partner and I had reached an agreement. Each of us would suggest three property management firms that would take on the day-to-day management duties until a dissolution was agreed upon. Accordingly, I began interviewing potential management companies.

I spoke to several. There were many candidates who seemed qualified, but one stood out more than the others and seemed to understand my situation best. Call her Mary Jane.

Mary Jane was the head of a well-known and respected management company. She and her firm were certainly qualified. Best of all, Mary related to me how she had stepped into a similar situation. In this previous experience, Mary didn't merely manage some properties on an interim basis. She claimed to be instrumental in restoring the frayed relationship between the two partners. I was distraught over the deteriorating friendship with my partner. It seemed like Mary Jane understood me better than any of the other candidates. When I heard her talking about how she restored the previous relationship, I said, "do that for me."

In the meantime, my case was grinding its way through the courts. A scheduling conference was next on the calendar. While I had been attending every court appointment, this one seemed so minor I almost skipped it. I decided to go at the last minute. I arrived at the courtroom early and waited in the hall for a previous case to finish. I was shocked to bump into Mary Jane. Not knowing any better, I asked her what she was doing there. The cold shoulder I got was my first clue I was in trouble.

I had just walked into an ambush. Instead of developing his own list of property management candidates, my partner had instead gotten a copy of mine. He proceeded to interview my candidates and had turned Mary Jane against me.

There was little time to think any of this through. Before I knew it, my case was called and what I thought was going to be a scheduling conference morphed into a hearing. Mary Jane was the first witness to testify. The dissertation of her credentials and accomplishments was lengthy. She was the head of this firm and the chairperson of that real estate industry organization. She claimed to have met me when I was a student in a real estate class she taught, thereby establishing her expertise as superior to mine. Just one problem—I had never been a student in any class taught by Mary Jane.

She was then asked her opinion about the best way to proceed with the property management question. She kept repeating, "it would be in the best interest of the real estate...," if I were essentially removed from the company I had founded. Then she went on to delicately explain what an incompetent rube I was.

It was certainly a hardball play by my partner and an incredible betrayal by Mary Jane. Worse still, a trusted employee had also defected and joined the mutiny. She testified against me too.

I was in big trouble. I needed to take the stand to get my side of the story in play. Ironically, just the day before in my regular Bible reading, I had read the passage in Matthew 10:19 NASB, "But when they hand you over, do not worry about how or what you are to say; for what you are to say will be given you in that hour." As I walked up to take the stand, I remember praying silently, "Lord, I really need that one to be true!"

I took the stand and was sworn in. My attorney and I had only a few minutes to prepare a list of questions he could ask me to get this problem back on track. Our Q&A session went well enough. Then the cross examination began.

My partner had a team of lawyers and they had obviously prepared in advance. There were stacks of yellow lined tablets on their table. Each of the tablets were full of questions they were determined to ask. They had made just one mistake.

Ordinarily, witnesses are deposed before live questioning in a courtroom. A deposition is usually conducted outside of court, often in a law firm conference room. The witness is sworn in and a court reporter records the testimony. By the time any questions are asked in court, the attorney has already heard the answers once before.

In their zeal to ambush me, my partner and his lawyers had skipped the deposition. They were hearing the answers to their questions for the first time. And the answers they were hearing were devastating to their cause. As my attorney later described it, "it was as if they kept stepping into the punch." They seemed determined to continue with their questioning, even while each answer was more detrimental than the last.

I was on the stand several hours that day without any preparation. Yet this was the day the case turned in my favor. What I needed to say certainly had been given to me just as the scriptures described. The judge made this concluding statement, "the only thing I can't give [Mr. Partner] which he seems to dearly want is to intentionally cause further harm to [Dave Decker]."

I had taken a Reality Face Punch right between the eyes and had not only survived, the other guy was the one prone on the canvas. Opposing counsel got a two-step refresher course in Lawyer 101: Never ask a question you do not already know the answer to. Two, the most dangerous lie in the courtroom is the one the client tells his own attorney.

Betrayal Part 2—In the Recovery Room

While a victory had been won, I was steamed about how Mary Jane had betrayed me. I wanted to feed her headfirst into a meat grinder. Check that, feet first would have been more painful. I thought of quite a few pithy things to say to her.

Perhaps the Lord protected me from myself. I never saw Mary Jane again.

In time, I began to realize my response was all wrong. Near the end of his life, Jesus was also put on trial. Dubious witnesses were called to make false accusations. Now I knew a little of what that may have felt like.

Accused of ridiculous charges, Jesus remained silent. Then He was taken away to be beaten and crucified. His physical suffering was indescribable, but the spiritual suffering was worse. Jesus was burdened with paying for the sins of all time all while being abandoned by God—"My God, My God, why have you forsaken me?" Matthew 27:46 NASB

Yet even when His suffering was at its peak, Jesus had this to say, "Father forgive them, for they do not know what they are doing." Luke 23:34 NASB

In other words, Jesus was like a defense attorney pleading a case before the Judge. Since his clients were obviously guilty, Jesus made the only plea for mercy he could—the guilty were ignorant of what they were doing. But Jesus was not just the defense attorney. He was the victim. He had the capacity to settle the score, but he sought mercy instead. He extended this extraordinary act of forgiveness not after taking time to think about it, but while His suffering was at its peak.

In all, it's beyond my comprehension. But one concept I could grasp was the need to let go of the wrong done to me.

How to Forgive

There are some crazy ideas about Christian forgiveness. The cliches roll off the tongue with ease—"forgive and forget." This concept is ridiculous. Nowhere in the Bible are Christians called upon to forgive and forget. God does not even do this. How can an all-knowing God forget some things?

Instead, God does not dwell on the things he has forgiven. "As far as the east is from the west, so far has He removed our wrongdoings from us." Psalm 103:12 NASB. I needed to do the same. I came up with a five-step process for forgiveness:

1. Understand that forgiveness is not optional, but rather a prerequisite to your own forgiveness. Mark 11:25 ESV says, "And whenever you stand praying, forgive, if you have anything against anyone, so that your Father also who is in heaven may forgive you your trespasses."

2. Disregard your feelings. Your injury may be physical or spiritual, but either way, the injury is very real. It's understandable to be upset about what has happened. God is well aware of these injustices, but calls upon us to forgive anyway, just as Jesus did. This is good medicine. We don't want bitterness to overcome us and take over our lives.

   > See to it that no one fails to obtain the grace of God; that no "root of bitterness" springs up and causes trouble, and by it many become defiled.
   > —Hebrews 12:15 ESV

3. Stop dwelling on the hurt. Put those thoughts as far as the east is from the west. Like many Christian principles, this is easy to understand but hard to implement. If you're like me, those thoughts can be unrelenting, tracking you down like a blood hound after prey. That's why you need to exercise the Power of Substitution. You can't just not think about something. When negative thoughts intrude, banish them by focusing on something more positive. Try this out:

> Finally, brothers, whatever is true, whatever is honorable, whatever is just, whatever is pure, whatever is lovely, whatever is commendable, if there is any excellence, if there is anything worthy of praise, think about these things.
>
> —Philippians 4:8 ESV

4. Stop entertaining thoughts of revenge. The Bible says in Romans 12:19, NASB: "Never take your own revenge, beloved, but leave room for the wrath of God, for it is written: 'vengeance is mine, I will repay,' says the Lord." Revenge takes the greatest toll on the one seeking it. Revenge is like preparing a poison for your adversary and then drinking it yourself. Better to focus your creativity on the next deal, the next opportunity or a new way to solve an old problem. That's the Power of Substitution again!

5. Pray for the one that hurt you. This is the hardest part of all. This is what Jesus did when he was on the cross praying, "Father forgive them, for they do not know what they are doing." I will admit my prayers for Mary

Jane were driven more by obedience than by enthusiasm. I did not know Mary Jane well and did not know how to pray for her specifically. Therefore, I prayed that she would enjoy good health and success and that the Lord would bless her according to her needs. And, of course, I prayed that she would accept Jesus as her Savior, if she had not already done so.

This is more than just some machinations from a hyperventilating real estate jockey. Consider what Jesus said in Matthew 5:43-47.

> You have heard that it was said, 'You shall love your neighbor and hate your enemy.' [44] But I say to you, Love your enemies and pray for those who persecute you, [45] so that you may be sons of your Father who is in heaven. For he makes his sun rise on the evil and on the good, and sends rain on the just and on the unjust. [46] For if you love those who love you, what reward do you have? Do not even the tax collectors do the same? [47] And if you greet only your brothers, what more are you doing than others? Do not even the Gentiles do the same?

Something to keep in mind in this equation is that the perpetrator in most cases won't be asking for forgiveness. You can skip the confrontation unless you want to hear them say, "I did nothing wrong." Forgiveness should still be extended. Christ extended forgiveness towards us before we ever asked. The greatest beneficiary of forgiveness is the victim, not the perpetrator. Having extending forgiveness, you are free to go on with your life. Your mind will be free from the revenge clutter and instead focused on enhancing your prosperity.

While it is helpful to study how to forgive, it is just as important to understand what forgiveness is not:

1. Forgiveness does not require us to forget. Most victims will not be able to do this even if they wanted. If you did forget what happened, that would give an opportunity to the offender to injure again. Not dwelling on the matter does not equate to forgetting.

2. Forgiveness does not require us to spare the offender from the consequences of their offense. Those consequences can range from damage to reputation to facing criminal charges and other severe consequences. Nor should victims feel guilty about the suffering of the offender because of these consequences.

3. Forgiveness does not require a restoration of personal relationships. Whether a romantic relationship or a business one, sometimes relationships must end. I really had no previous relationship with Mary Jane. I met her only once before. Not when I was a student in her class, but when she showed me an apartment building for sale. That I never saw her again after our court appearance was not something I planned. If I were to bump into Mary Jane today, I would greet her as if nothing had ever happened. I am not ashamed to say that I would never do business with Mary Jane again, even though I feel I have forgiven her. Of course, things don't have to be all or nothing. While some relationships must end,

other relationships can still move forward under greater constraints or changed expectations.

One last kernel of wisdom to consider: The perpetrator may never have intended to inflict all the hurt you experienced. Perhaps for them, it was just another day at the office. You may be ruminating in pain and they don't even remember. These folks may not be worth the mental energy. If you view them as adversaries, then continuing to stew on this hands them another win.

A Reality Face Punch Epilogue

Time also has a way of healing and taking the edge off the injury as an epilogue to this story will bear out. In the wake of that court appearance, I immediately fired the employee who betrayed me. Years later, I got a call from an employer seeking a reference for this former associate. I set aside my experience and gave her a good recommendation.

My partner and I were able to settle out of court. We divided hundreds of apartments in half. In time, my former partner sold his buildings and moved out of the area.

I was able to grow my real estate holdings more than ten-fold to the 1,200 apartments I have today.

Mary Jane eventually stepped down from leading the property management company and relocated out of the area, marking what appears to be semi-retirement. Ironically, she offers her services as an expert witness in real estate litigation.

I have wondered if Mary's assertion that I was a student in one of her classes was an outright lie or an honest mistake. If a lie, it was a foolish one easily refuted. To the best of my knowledge, the classes she taught were small in size. Could it really be she was so uninvolved with her students that she would mistake me for one of them? This is something I will never know. What I do know is that Mary Jane testified under oath to something that wasn't true and she stood to profit from that testimony.

It is worth reviewing Romans 12:19, NASB again: "Never take your own revenge, beloved, but leave room for the wrath of God, for it is written: 'vengeance is mine, I will repay,' says the Lord."

I know too little about what happened to me to know why it happened. Better to leave vengeance to the Lord. Even the Old Testament concept of an eye for an eye and a tooth for a tooth is still helpful. Not taken literally. Then we would all be blind and toothless. However, we can accept the concept as an instruction in restraint. Notice in the face of my injury, I wanted to feed Mary Jane into a meat grinder! Our human nature is not only to retaliate but also to escalate. The punishment should fit the crime.

The most important thing to take away from this whole experience is that I survived to a new day where I could thrive. Which isn't to say this was the only time I employed my face as a shield. To find out about that, continue to The Reality Face Punch Part Two, Cue Up My Face for Another Punch in the Nose.

We are afflicted in every way, but not crushed; perplexed, but not driven to despair; persecuted, but not forsaken; struck down, but not destroyed.

—2 Corinthians 4:8-9 ESV

"Good judgment is the result of experience, and experience the result of bad judgment."

—Mark Twain

5

THE REALITY FACE PUNCH (PART 2)

I survived one Reality Face Punch in the last chapter just in time to sustain another.

In 2003, my real estate operation was much smaller. There were just two of us in the office—me and my wife. She was expecting our first child and was transitioning to being a stay-at-home mom. I had to find a new assistant. That's how we came to know Slippery Sue. Obviously, that's not her real name.

Sue was smart, efficient and capable. She made a great assistant, except for the stealing. It began with Sue requesting an advance on her payroll. I never turned down a request. Then she started to "borrow" on her own. Initially, she repaid the loans. Then it got away from her.

In those days, we sometimes had to offer an incentive to rent apartments. That incentive was often the first month rent free. Sue booked every apartment as having the first month free, even when we weren't offering the special. In those instances, she kept the first month's rent for herself. I discovered a single instance of manipulation early and confronted Sue on a Friday. She had a tearful explanation and begged to keep her job. I told her I would need the weekend to think it over. Her remorse seemed genuine.

I sought wide ranging advice. It's interesting how the advice broke down demographically. Nearly every Christian advisor suggested I fire her. Women who weighed in also unanimously favored termination. My pastor recommended dismissal. Only other guys in a similar predicament to me had mercy. I sought the advice of several other landlords running one-man operations with a single assistant, like myself. They were also unanimous—find a way to keep her.

I let her keep her job. I warned of the consequences should she steal again. Not only would she lose her job, she would be turned over to law enforcement.

That crunching noise you're hearing is the sound of a fist hitting my face.

We went back to work and Sue went right back to stealing. It would be two years before I discovered the theft the second time.

Sue and I worked alone in an office together for a total of five years. She was a personable, friendly person. Often on a Monday, she would chat me up about what her kids had been up to over the weekend and ask about my kids. Then she would return to her desk and steal from me.

In June 2008, I was dealing with a tenant who had a past-due balance. I confronted the tenant about the balance. The tenant disputed the amount that was past due and indicated that she had receipts to support her claim. Adrenaline started coursing through my body.

There had been plenty of signs that suggested Slippery Sue was not a good manager of her personal finances. She was an Olympic shopper. If I ever needed something from the mall, she knew where to get it, where to park and when it was likely to be on sale.

I was frequently out of the office on appointments. I recall returning to the office to find Sue in tears. She had just learned that her husband had lost his job. I felt terrible for Sue. The same day, on her lunch hour, Sue went out and bought a car! She said that she wanted to secure the automobile loan before the credit reporting agencies figured out her husband was unemployed.

There was another day when a lunch time trip to the mall tallied $700 in less than an hour by her own admission. Sue had a daughter in private skating lessons. Slippery was out of work for a few days owing to a "minor medical procedure," which turned out to be breast implants.

All these thoughts rushed through my mind as I considered the tenant's claim that her rental account balance was inaccurate. I decided to meet the tenant at her home to get a copy of the receipt. I didn't want the tenant coming into the office and Slippery Sue being tipped off to what I knew or was trying to discover. I obtained a copy of the receipt. The receipt was signed by Slippery Sue and corroborated the tenant's claim. The payment wasn't recorded in our books.

I knew I had a problem. I began reviewing the books and records to identify any additional discrepancies. I decided to discretely advertise Slippery Sue's job. I wanted to get a running start on finding her replacement. Apparently, I wasn't as discreet as I thought.

"Are you advertising my job?" she asked me a day later.

I admitted I was and explained why. Then I fired her. Before she left, I made her an offer.

"Anything you confess to today is just between you and me. But after today, anything that I find that you haven't confessed to, I go to the police with."

Sue confessed to a couple of additional instances of theft. However, I had already been aware of them from my preliminary investigation.

She left and over the coming days, I continued to investigate. I found more instances of theft. I decided a phone call to Sue was in order.

"Sue, I've found more instances of theft. I'm not going to tell you what I've found, but I am going to tell you again. Anything you confess to now is just between us. If you continue to maintain your silence, you will be explaining what I've found to the police."

Now Sue faced a dilemma. She knew something I did not. She knew the theft was widespread and had been going on for years. I had yet to discover this. She knew the theft was extensive. What she didn't know was the specific instances I had found. She decided to guess. She did not guess well.

She confessed to a few more instances of theft, but I already knew about them. I told her there were more that I had found that she had not admitted to. She insisted that was all she could remember.

As I continued to investigate, I found still more evidence of stealing. My investigation was far from complete, but it was time to call the police.

The responding officer, Ryan Golomski, was young with short straw-colored hair and an athletic build. He was exceptionally compassionate. We sat at my conference table and went over the details.

"I'm so sorry you've had this experience Mr. Decker," he repeated several times.

Our meeting happened to be on a payroll Friday. Ordinarily, Slippery Sue would have had a final paycheck coming. But the degree of theft I had discovered exceeded her payroll and there would be no paycheck for Slippery Sue. I had not had the opportunity to share that fact with Sue yet. So as fate would have it, Slippery Sue came into the office to collect her final paycheck while I was meeting with Officer Golomski!

Of course, I introduced her.

"Officer, please meet Slippery Sue, the perpetrator."

It was as if Golomski flipped some kind of switch in his being. Officer Friendly disappeared in an instant, replaced by Lieutenant Authority. Golomski sat Sue down at the conference table and remained standing. He leaned into her personal space and asked a series of questions. Slippery wasn't denying anything.

Then the officer had a question for me.

"Are you willing to prosecute?"

"Please don't do this," begged Sue.

My heart was pounding. I felt sick. I looked at Sue. I looked at the officer. I said I would prosecute.

"I'm satisfied that a crime has been committed, please stand up and clasp your hands behind your back," came the order.

Sue stood up and Officer Golomski placed her in handcuffs.

"Please, I was on my way to pick up my kids. Will you call my babysitter and have her pick up my kids?" pleaded Sue.

I said I would and she gave me the number. The officer escorted Sue out of my office. I called the baby-sitter.

"Sue had something come up. She won't be able to get the kids, can you get them and watch them for a few hours?"

The baby-sitter said she would.

Slippery Sue received a municipal citation and was released later that day.

In the coming days, I continued the investigation. I discovered an accordion file of unpaid bills. I spread the bills out on Sue's desk. But Sue's desk wasn't big enough. I began to spread the bills out on the floor. Unpaid bills lined the perimeter of the entire three-office suite.

I started with the oldest bills first and began bringing everything up to date. I owed a lot of money. Things were tight, but I survived. I began to dig out of the pit I was in.

As the investigation progressed, I found more instances of theft. It was like death by a thousand cuts.

Sue was thorough about covering her tracks. She had discarded leases and applications when those documents contradicted our financial records. Ultimately, I used this deception to my advantage. Whenever I discovered a file with a lease or an application missing, I knew there was likely an instance of theft associated with it. To prove the case, I had to recover those documents. By then, some of the tenants had moved. Some had even been evicted! I never recovered everything, but I recovered most of the missing documents.

The investigation encroached on some family time, some church services and activities. I could only work on the investigation sporadically while attending to usual business. The inquiry took 10 months to complete. The result was two massive three ring binders that would stack about two feet tall.

Time to call the police again. In no time, I was meeting with Detective Mark Gralinski. Detective Gralinski looked like he just stepped out of central casting for a police detective. He had short hair, a no-nonsense demeanor and a conservative grey suit. He seemed like a nice guy, genuinely concerned. He wasn't in a rush and was patient with my many questions. I turned my binders over and he promised to get back to me.

Shortly later, Detective Gralinski called me into the station for further questioning. We sat down in a stark interview room. I think the walls of that room were used to hearing some drama. The detective indicated that my evidence was complete and self-explanatory. There was just one question he wanted to ask.

"Where you romantically involved with this woman?"

I stated not only was I not involved, but also that I had outlined several precautions on her first day of employment. Sue was an attractive woman about the same age as my wife. I thought it best if we always kept the office door open. This way, our privacy would be limited. I also explained that if we were going somewhere, we would take separate cars. And there would be no lunches together unless her husband or my wife was present.

Satisfied, the detective indicated they would be picking Sue up and charging her with a felony related to theft through employment.

I fired Sue in June of 2008. My investigation was spread over 10 months. By the time Sue was charged with the felony, it was February 2010. Her case wound through the courts. I had several meetings with Assistant District Attorney Tim Westphal, who oversaw the prosecution of my case.

ADA Westphal was an ideal public servant. He had a workmen like approach. I remember him as a dedicated individual professionally attired but unconcerned about his appearance. His suit was rumpled and his black dress shoes worn. But he knew his trade, he worked hard and kept me informed.

I remember a beautiful summer Saturday that I was at a park with my kids. This case was the furthest thing from my mind. I received a call from Tim, who updated me on the latest details of the case. I was enjoying a perfect summer day, Tim was tirelessly pursing justice on my behalf.

Sue cut a plea deal. I was aware of the details of the plea bargain and thought it was fair. Sue would be required to make restitution for the stolen money and serve four months of detention with work release privileges. Attorney Westphal warned me that the defense could still argue for a lesser sentence and probably would.

I thought I had this all figured out. The defense would argue for a reduced sentence. Tim would be in favor of the plea bargain. I would give a victim's impact statement calling for a far harsher penalty. Then the judge would balance everything out and go with the plea bargain.

That's not what happened.

Sentencing was December 9, 2010 before Judge Lloyd Carter. Attorney Westphal and I were making small talk waiting for the case to be called. We talked about whether there was any joy in seeing someone suffer the consequences of their actions. We both agreed there was not.

The defense argued as anticipated, noting that this type of crime had a low recidivism rate. Attorney Westphal walked everyone through the process of how the plea agreement was reached and why it was considered fair. Then I made my impassioned statement.

There was an assessment report from probation and parole. Then Judge Carter rendered his verdict.

Judge Carter seemed incensed. He went on a tear. He chewed Sue out, calling her a con man and a thief. He chewed me out! He said, "If you catch someone stealing, you fire them the first time." He compared this circumstance to other offenders he had sentenced, including a lawyer that had stolen from some clients. In the middle of the dissertation, he mentioned that Sue was going to lose her freedom.

By now, I was sweating! I have no idea what this must have been like for Sue.

Judge Carter even found fault with the assessment from probation and parole. Sue had filed bankruptcy in the past and the report noted that it seemed as if Sue had failed to learn anything from the shame of having to file bankruptcy.

"Anyone find a problem with this report?" Judge Carter inquired.

No one responded. Judge Carter answered his own question:

"The purpose of a bankruptcy proceeding is to discharge the debts of the debtor, and nothing more. Inflicting shame is not an objective of a bankruptcy filing."

In making this observation, in my unqualified opinion, Judge Carter was slamming the door on a loophole for any potential appeal.

Then Sue had the opportunity to make a statement. I was sitting behind Sue, several rows back. Sue stood, turned and faced me. "I am sorry" she said haltingly, each word like a single sentence. Tears were streaming. I'd roughed her up pretty well with my statement, and that was a side of me she wasn't used to seeing. Perhaps she thought I had changed from the experience, becoming bitter. She reflected on that idea and added, "I'm responsible for that change too."

Ultimately, the sentence handed down by Judge Carter was tougher than what any of us had asked for, including me.

Sue was ordered to make restitution and received a 30-day jail sentence, followed by seven months of work release. During work release, Sue would be locked up at night but would be allowed out of jail for 50 hours per week to continue her new job. There was no allowance made for child-care duties and Sue had four young children.

Sue was ineligible for early release through good behavior. Sue had made a down payment toward her restitution, and Judge Carter ordered that 40% of her net wages be dedicated to paying the remaining balance. Additionally, there was five years of probation.

Sue was remanded to custody immediately. I saw her walked off in handcuffs for a second time. She would be spending Christmas and New Year's in jail. She wouldn't sleep in her own bed again for eight months.

I walked out of the court room and saw Sue's husband conferring with their attorney. The husband was in tears. And Sue's troubles were far from over.

Sue had been involved in several charitable organizations, but always as the treasurer or ticket taker, responsible for managing the cash box. Sue served as the treasurer for a suburban kid's soccer club. Knowing this, I called the president of the soccer club and left a message.

"Your treasurer used to be my employee and has been charged with a felony for theft through employment. Call me if you'd like to know more."

I thought it odd that I never got a return call. Turns out, Sue and the president were both stealing from the soccer club!

Sue was eventually charged with stealing $12,690 from the soccer club. The president stole more than $70,000!

Soccer Moms stealing like a modern-day Bonnie and Clyde was too irresistible for the media, and Sue got herself on the local TV news.

Needing to make restitution to reduce sentencing on the new charges, Sue's restitution payments to me started to wane. Therefore, her parole was extended. Sue made a final restitution payment to me in 2018, 10 years after I fired her. She had been on probation since sentencing, nearly nine years instead of five.

In 2021, Sue petitioned her husband for divorce.

Tim Westphal was right. There was no joy in any of this.

Inserting My Face into Heavy Fist Traffic

We can't leave this topic without me sharing the times the Reality Face Punch resulted in an actual punch in the face. I was a little younger then. I like to say that when I was young, I was young and foolish. Now, I am no longer young!

There was a kid a year older living in the neighborhood who had a beef with me. Let's call him Biff. I can't remember what the conflict was about. But one summer at a Little League Baseball game when I was in about the eighth grade, we set about settling the score.

I don't recall how the dust up got started. Luckily, I deftly blocked all his punches with my face. A black eye was the result.

That bruise had nearly healed when I ran into the problem again. I had a morning paper route and one of my best friends had an afternoon route. I often helped my friend deliver his papers. Biff was on the afternoon route at the back of a cul-de-sac.

I was helping deliver the papers when Biff, his older brother and another neighborhood kid were playing basketball in Biff's driveway. I saw them from a distance from my newspaper delivery bicycle. I had to decide what to do. I decided to play it cool and deliver the paper like nothing was wrong.

They decided to play it otherwise.

The details aren't important. Let's just say it was a day I would rather forget.

But time can be a funny thing. Shortly after I graduated high school, the older brother was killed in an automobile accident. I was shocked and saddened to hear this. He certainly didn't deserve that for anything he did to me.

More time went by, decades in fact. A multi-year high school reunion was scheduled. It's one of those occasions when you start to think, "what ever happened to …."

There were lots of people more interesting to me than Biff. But eventually, I got around to conducting an internet search on him as well. That's when I learned for the first time that Biff was two years ahead of me, not one.

Turns out, Biff and I had nearly an identical trajectory. We both attended business school at the same large state university.

We both left our home state to pursue employment. We both started our own companies.

But there, things begin to diverge. Biff eventually returned to our home state. I have not. He remained a big fan of Indiana sports teams while I have moved on. I know all these things because they were included in Biff's obituary. He was 59 when he died.

Biff had been quite a lady's man in high school. Yet the obituary didn't include the names of a wife or any children. The company Biff started seemed to have expired when he did. If there is a way to leave this world without leaving a ripple on the water, Biff may have found it.

Signing Up for Another Face Punch

There was one other occasion when I seemed determined to insert my face in heavy fist traffic. I was in high school. There was a kid who was always out for trouble. Maybe you could say he was a bully. Mostly, he left me alone. Until he didn't.

Once again, I don't remember how the conflict started. But honor required that a fight after school be scheduled.

I don't know why fights always seemed to take place behind the church across the street from the high school. But it was universally understood that if you were challenged to "meet me at the church after school," you knew you wouldn't be playing cards or engaging in Bible study.

Going across the street to the church didn't do any good. The school held they maintained jurisdiction over student conduct until they arrived home. If caught fighting behind the church on the way home from school, you could count on a three-to-five-day suspension. During the suspension, you would not be allowed to make up any assignments or tests and would receive a failing grade instead.

Once I agreed to that fight, I spent the rest of the day sick with worry. I was certain I would be caught. My grades were important to me and they were likely to be compromised. I would be in trouble at school, my parents would be mad at me, and worst of all, I was going to get beat up!

Nevertheless, when school let out, I made a beeline for the church. I felt like a dead man walking, but I didn't want to be counted a coward.

When I arrived, there were already six or eight kids waiting to see a fight. I don't know how they found out. I certainly didn't want any witnesses to my undoing. Sometimes, there are no secrets.

The bully wasn't there yet, so I did my best to talk tough and look confident. And then I waited.

I wish I could tell you that when that bully showed up, I laid him out with the first punch. I wish I could report that I warned him that if he ever hassled me again, he'd get it again only worse.

But nothing like that ever happened. The bully never showed.

I paced around sounding tough and tried to seem thoroughly disgusted that I didn't get a chance to punch him in the nose. Then I stomped off relieved that my life had been spared!

If this was a Hollywood ending, I'd be able to tell you that the bully never bothered me again. But this is real life. I still was subject to the occasional snarky comment, but things were toned down to an acceptable chatter.

I learned a good lesson about barking, biting and bullies. Since then, I've learned that there are plenty of bullies lurking out there that never grew up. They don't get my heart beating anymore. There's no need to be angry.

I'm a landlord and the landlord tenant relationship isn't always smooth. Yet 99% or more of our residents fit nicely within the Goodwill Paradox. They're nice people who want to do the right thing. I have 1,200 apartments and I manage 500 more for clients. If 1% of the residents gave me a hard time that would be 17 people. It's nowhere near that, often only one or two or even none.

Yet within that tiny minority of folks, I've been threatened a few times. Some wanted to sue me, others were going to burn my building down. None have ever torched a property and few have ever sued.

That's not to say that business is easy. Sometimes, just a single punch in the face would make for a calm day. I've had days when two buildings miles apart caught fire on the same day—by accident, not by arson!

Reality Face Punch Lessons

Painful lessons can be a good teacher. Shortly after firing Slippery Sue, growth enabled us to hire two employees to perform the work that Sue had previously done. This way, duties could be divided to require collusion to steal. In all, our approach to security is much more sophisticated now.

While the occasional Reality Face Punch probably cannot be avoided, most entrepreneurial warriors can still survive and thrive.

Detective Gralinski shared with me that employee theft is more common than most people realize. Since those days, it seems like every week local news reports include an account of an employee charged with theft from their employer. If you own a retail store, shoplifting is part of operating reality. Even worse, the folks most dangerous to retail operations are often the store employees. The very people you see daily and trust and work with side by side can sometimes be counted on to steal from you. When it happens, it feels like a punch in the face. That's the Reality Face Punch.

Punching Back

But there's more to the Reality Face Punch than merely ducking blows. There is the opportunity to deliver a few punches of our own. Not literally of course, but rhetorically.

You may not be a salesperson, but everyone is in the persuasion game. Whether it be convincing that special someone about a date, or even marriage, to making the case for a raise or promotion, to getting the job in the first place or convincing a teenager to clean up their room, we're all in the persuasion business. And in the face of ever shrinking attention spans, there may only be one shot at this, so it had better be good. Time to deliver a rhetorical face punch.

Whenever possible, try to reduce the argument to a single sentence that entirely changes the game. Call it a sound bite. Examples will be helpful. In the chapter on The Future of Autonomous Vehicles, I counter the claim that autonomous vehicles will be the undoing of the automobile industry. Supposed experts believe that we will all be subscribers to ride-sharing services, and individual automobile ownership will decline precipitously, leading to the implosion of the industry. This argument notes that our cars are idle most of the time—parked somewhere taking up space.

Nice thinking, but here's the Realty Face Punch: For the first time in recorded history, a product or service will become easier to use, but we will want less of it. Wrong. There will be more cars, not less.

Just for good measure, I follow that jab to the nose with a crisp hook to the jaw. There's a certain yuck factor to anything shared. Our cars likely spend most of their time idle. However, that doesn't mean I'm interested in being transported in a public-access vehicle. My toothbrush spends most of its time sitting in a glass by my sink, but that doesn't mean I want to participate in a toothbrush sharing service. Pow, another punch to the face!

It doesn't hurt to inject a little humor while punching away. For now, my face is worn out, please read on!

Blessed is the man who remains steadfast under trial, for when he has stood the test he will receive the crown of life, which God has promised to those who love him.

—James 1:12 ESV

"

"Far better it is to dare mighty things, to win glorious triumphs, even though checkered by failure . . . than to rank with those timid spirits who neither enjoy much nor suffer much."

—Theodore Roosevelt

"

6

ROOKIE SEASON

If your rookie season is only supposed to be one year, then let me say it's been a long year. I might still be a rookie. I'm certainly still learning. In those early years, the lessons came fast and furious.

Right out of college, I landed a job with a big Fortune 500 company. Let's call it Company Big. It was a second choice. I wanted to go into real estate, but it was 1985. The tax laws were changing in a way unfavorable to real estate. There were few jobs to be had. I settled for the next best thing.

My experiences at Company Big rendered a constant state of flux. When I started and during my entire tenure, Big was always laying off. My first day, as I toured the facility, I over-heard employees grumbling about who would be next to get the axe.

I participated in a financial management training program that rotated trainees through various roles every six months. We took Company Big training courses in the evenings. Exams were challenging. Tests were timed. You had to write furiously without pause to complete within the allotted period. I believe anything less than 80% was a failing grade. Post a failing average and you lost your job.

My training class consisted of two men, including me, and one woman, all Caucasians. One of the guys did not make the grade and got shown the door. There was an African American woman in a class ahead who likewise was in academic trouble. Management rescored her exams to find the points to restore her standing.

One of the job rotations involved an assignment in England. That sounded fascinating, so I put myself in contention. I finished second in that contest. The decision-making process was slow. Try joining a health club or even renewing an apartment lease if you anticipate moving overseas soon. Living in a state of flux is hard. Not getting the job, harder.

One of my instructors was a woman in middle management. She was a vigorous advocate for women in Company Big. Periodically, positions would become available throughout the company, and any qualified person could apply and interview for the position. It was understood when this woman was the hiring manager, no men need apply.

I was in a class with mostly women taught by this female manager. Later, shortly after the class was over, we attended a larger meeting where the same woman was speaking. She discussed the class and started to count off the attendees on her fingers—mentioning all the female students and leaving me out. After the meeting we were mingling, making small talk. This manager approached me and apologized for not mentioning me, saying, "I'm sorry, Dave. When I look into a room, I only see the women."

One of my rotations was on the corporate audit staff. I was given the assignment of auditing travel and living expense reimbursement reports to determine whether our sales staff had followed procedures regarding treatment of government employees. Company Big including the federal government among its customers. There were stringent government regulations about when hospitality crossed the line from mere kindness to a bribe. What might be common practice in the private sector could be verboten with government workers.

I was led to believe the audit was confidential. Or at least I will offer that as my excuse. Somehow, my clumsy interactions with the salesforce led to me frightening some of them half to death. At the time, Arnold Schwarzeneger starred in a movie as an oppressive cyborg. That's how I gained the nickname "The Terminator."

Auditing the travel and living reimbursement reports often required me to contact individual salespeople to gain clarification about these interactions with government employees. But explaining all that took some time. Often, I would begin the telephone conversation by saying, "This is Dave Decker with the corporate audit staff, and I am reviewing your travel and living statement from [date]."

Before I could go on to further explain my purpose, the confessions would begin! One salesman interrupted me, saying that if there was any discrepancy, I should just tell him the amount and he would immediately reimburse the company. I probably should have stepped in and explained the reason for my inquiry sooner. But they didn't call me The Terminator for nothing!

Another overseas opportunity came up in Japan. Three were invited to apply, two women and yours truly. One of the ladies dropped out by her own fruition. That just left me and the other woman, who happened to be my ex-girlfriend. Being my ex-girlfriend was her idea, not mine.

We interviewed with the top brass at Company Big, including leadership from Japan. The guy from Japan had more dandruff flakes on his suit jacket than the snow on Mount Fuji.

The day came to make the big decision. I was called into the office of the Manager of Finance, the top financial manager of our division. He was from England and spoke with a British accent. Having this man as a mentor and advocate could lead to a meteoric career.

I sat down at a conference table in his enormous office. I glanced out the window at the panorama of his daily view. Quite an upgrade from the bland beige of my cubie walls. He sat down and wasted no time explaining the verdict.

"Here at Company Big, we're looking for three things. Smarts, drive, and fire in the belly. And I really don't see any of those things in you." That sounds even more cutting when delivered in a clipped British accent.

I admit I wasn't prepared for an assessment like that. So I squared my jaw, sat up straight, leaned forward, looked him straight in the eye and said, "does that mean I don't get the job?"

Other responses that were rejected:

1. Maybe so, but I bet I can kick your butt at Pac Man.
2. Why do people from England talk so funny?
3. But really, how do you like me so far?

It didn't seem quite as funny at the time. I figured my Company Big career was over. It would take a few years to appreciate the wisdom and favor that had been extended to me that day. I had already been thinking about how to transition into a career in real estate. All I needed was a good shove. I considered myself shoved.

As much as I hate to admit it, I think Mr. English's assessment was correct. Not that I was a lazy dolt, but Company Big had yet to see my best. For that to happen, I would have to start my own company.

I remember a one-on-one meeting I had with a Company Big middle manager. He was tall and lanky and nearing retirement. He had short, wavy grey hair, silver-rimmed glasses to match, and a plentiful mustache. After we completed the purpose for our meeting, we began talking shop. He leaned back in his chair, propped his feet on his desk and started tracing the highlights of his career. This was a man that was clearly pleased with himself and all he had accomplished. My only thought was, "if I don't get out of here, this is going to be me in 30 years."

I began to reach out to the local real estate community. Somehow, I wormed my way into an interview at the Trammel Crow Company. Trammel Crow is a prestigious national developer and highly respected. Their offices were in one of their recent developments on the northwest side of Milwaukee. The buildings are a square combination of steel and glass, reminiscent of a flash cube from an old-fashioned analog camera.

My interview began with a couple of younger associates. I must have passed the audition, because I was instructed to stick around a bit longer. The people I met with next were increasingly older. Yet the verdict here was not what I wanted either. The most senior manager congratulated me on making it as far as I did. He explained that they only hire MBAs. I only had an undergraduate degree. They didn't even make a practice of interviewing undergrads.

Another swing and a miss. It was a disappointment at the time, but once again, fortune was smiling my way. The lease up on those office towers didn't play out as intended. Those same managers that declined my candidacy were later named as defendants in the foreclosure. Trammell Crow continues to thrive throughout the US and Europe. But they are no longer in Milwaukee.

I had been looking for apartment buildings to buy. I quickly grew frustrated with the opportunities real estate agents were bringing me. I started driving around noting the addresses of apartment buildings I was interested in buying. I would discretely call the assessor's office during my workday to inquire who owned these buildings. It was the only research tool available to me in the days before the internet.

I had no idea what I was doing or who I was calling. One of the building owners I called on was a partnership between two men unfamiliar to me, whom I will refer to as Steve and Craig. I called the Craig's residence and spoke to Craig's wife. I think we talked at least an hour. She indicated that her husband handled property management, and his partner, Steve, handled buying and selling. She suggested I call Steve and I did.

I told Mr. Steve I was interested in buying one of his apartment buildings. He suggested we have lunch. We met for lunch in a restaurant that also happened to be one of Mr. Steve's tenants in a mixed-use building he owned. The property was mostly apartments, but also some commercial space, including the restaurant.

We sat down and got acquainted. I was still too inexperienced to know that Steve and Craig were the founders of one of the largest real estate companies in the area. We never got around to discussing me buying any of their apartment buildings. Instead, what I got was a two-hour real estate indoctrination. I felt as if I had just sat for an intensive final exam. I wish I had recorded the conversation for study later. I got advice about buying real estate. Steve shared with me how he got started. He gave me the name of his banker and suggested I call him next. It was an incredible opportunity.

I kept waiting for the lunch check to arrive. It never did. Steve had an understanding with the restaurant proprietor, who was also his tenant, and he picked up the tab. With travel time, I had played hooky from Company Big for about three hours.

I did call the banker as Steve suggested, Pat M. I received another invitation to lunch, this time at a white-tablecloth corporate dining facility. Pat was also gracious with his time and advice.

I continued calling apartment building owners, telling them I was interested in buying their property. Now and then, I would score an appointment to meet with an owner to look at his building. I would sneak out again during my lunch to look at these properties.

On one of these appointments, just as I was leaving another guy was arriving. He was a big guy, at least 6'5" and 300 pounds. The kind of guy you would remember.

The next day, I had another lunchtime apartment appointment. I wrapped up the meeting and started to leave when there was that same big guy, all 300 pounds. We got to talking.

The big guy was Bill T., a real estate broker specializing in apartment buildings. Our conversations led to me eventually joining his firm as a real estate agent. People at Company Big thought I had lost my mind. Maybe they were right. In my first year with Mr. T., I earned a third less than what I earned at Company Big.

As much as my report on Company Big must sound like the machinations of an old grump, I appreciated the opportunity I had at Big. I would employ later much of what I learned there.

Bill T. remains, to this day, one of the smartest and most creative real estate minds I have ever met. But working for him was an adventure. I started with Bill on December 7, 1987, Pearl Harbor Day. Earlier in the decade, a deep real estate recession had occurred, and Bill had been caught in it. He had a partner that filed for bankruptcy. Bill honorably stuck it out and tried to fulfill his obligations. Bill was also a landlord, but perhaps owing to the earlier financial distress, a cash strapped landlord.

Therefore, when the phone rang, it might be an investor interested in buying property. But it could also be an angry tenant upset about the lack of maintenance or an upset creditor wondering when they will be paid. This was in the days before caller ID and answering the phone was like a game of Russian Roulette.

Then there were the death rides. Bill would take individuals in the office with him on the way to various appointments. During the drive, he would berate the passenger with their incompetence. I can't say he was always wrong, but it was a tough way to learn. When it was my turn, I wanted to bail out of the car. I started developing ulcers in my mouth from the stress.

In those days, I thought if I could get a deal close but not be able to finish a transaction, Bill would step in and work his magic. Perhaps that thought served as a security blanket. I never actually employed the tactic, at least not until near the end of my time with Bill.

There was a young couple that was contemplating the purchase of an apartment building. I had gotten the deal inches away from acceptance, but not quite all the way home. I had exhausted myself and my ability and still no acceptance. Time to call in the calvary. Time to call in Big Bill.

I called a meeting between the four of us, the couple, Bill and myself. Then I turned the conversation over to Bill. I sat back with a smug look on my face. And Bill started the conversation by cutting the commission! It was all I could do to maintain consciousness. I was always hearing about how weak we were, how the commission was sacrosanct. Bill led off with cutting the commission without even trying to close the deal otherwise.

I could have done that. That is when I knew it was time to leave.

I started looking for office space. I had one criterion. Cheap. I found an ideal setup. A design-build architectural firm had some surplus space and was willing to rent a single office to me very reasonably. The deal came with access to copy and fax machines, office furniture, phones and a receptionist to answer them. A deal too good to be true.

I moved in on May 10, 1990, during a snowstorm. Once the commotion of moving and setting up was resolved, I sat alone in my new office. The quiet was deafening. I thought, "what have I done?"

There was no time to indulge my anxiety. There were bills to pay. Time to get busy.

Real estate listings for property for sale are contracts that belong to the brokerage firm named when the contract was created. In other words, real estate agents cannot take any existing business with them when they leave. I was starting from zero.

However, I knew that an apartment building was going to be sold because its owner had passed away. The property title was in the name of an estate and the executor of the estate was an attorney named Gerald Howitzer (not his real name). I had never heard of this attorney and had no idea who he was.

When I looked up his number, I noticed that his name was part of the law firm's name, Howitzer and Payne (again not the real name, but fun to talk about). That was my first hint that I was dealing with a big shot. I was just 27 at the time and my new company, Decker Properties, was just days old. I knew better than to just call this guy. I might never make it past the secretary.

So I began to do research. Remember, this is before the internet. I went to the central library. Before long, I learned Gerald Howitzer was a founding partner of one of the largest law firms in Wisconsin. I learned where Mr. Howitzer went to school and who was in his graduating class. I was looking for a name I recognized in his class that I could call for an introduction. But I recognized no one.

In desperation, I started calling all the people I knew that were about the same age as Gerald Howitzer. It didn't take me long before I was talking to my friend Walt at South Town Bank (another fake name). I will never forget Walt's answer when I asked him if he knew Gerald Howitzer. "Sure, I know Jerry."

That sounded like music to me. Walt offered to write a letter on my behalf. Email was not around yet. Walt even sent me a copy. Had my mother written this thing it would not have been as nice.

The next thing you know, I was in the swank downtown offices of Howitzer and Payne making my pitch. I had prepared my presentation on a personal computer, and those were new too. I know my competitors were also making their presentations, but those guys were old school. I had carefully documented my analysis with a rent study, comparable sales and cash flow projections all shown in a professional manner. My presentation would run circles around anything that came out of an old-fashioned typewriter.

One way or another, I got the listing. I found the buyer too. Naturally, when it was time to secure financing for the deal, I introduced the buyer to Walt at South Town Bank.

All an introduction gets you is a chance to perform. You still have to deliver. But I did and Walt did, so we closed the deal at South Town Bank. It was the largest commission I had earned up until that time. The financial pressure was off.

I recall an appointment I had with Gerald Howitzer, as we were negotiating a counteroffer or attending to another aspect of the transaction. I thought we were starting to really get along, so I asked him, "do you go by Jerry or do you prefer Gerald?" Without looking up from the file, he replied in a deep, steady baritone, "I prefer to be called Mr. Howitzer."

Sometimes you miss even when you're winning!

But I still got that commission. That was over 30 years ago. Gerald Howitzer has passed away since. I still appreciate the opportunity that was extended to me and the chance he took on a rookie. I was the recipient of abundant kindness from Steve, Craig and so many others.

Years later, I was even fixed up on a blind date with Craig's daughter. She is a delightful person. That was another occasion when I failed to pass the audition.

But it wasn't just my love life that was on the rocks. One weekend early on, I got a call at home from the landlord where I had my office. "Come get your stuff, I'm locking you out."

I was shocked. I didn't understand how this could be. I had been paying my rent to the design-build firm from which I was subletting. Turns out, they had not been paying their rent to the landlord.

I should have been more suspicious. The receptionist quit one day and was never replaced. More offices at the firm started going empty. One of the architects asked me if I knew anyone else that needed office space. But I was too busy to think through connecting any of those dots.

None of that mattered. I said to the building owner, "what do I do now?"

"Go and see Sandy on the third floor. She has a secretarial support service just for guys like you."

That is what I did—after collecting my stuff out of the old office.

Sure enough, Sandy was just who the landlord said she was. She was on the stocky side with a short haircut and the demeanor of a mellowed-out drill sergeant. But she had space at my price point—cheap. This time, no furniture was included.

No matter, I journeyed to the big-box office supply store across the street and acquired some assemble-it-yourself furniture. I assure you, it was only the finest, imported pictures of wood over particle board money can buy. Imported from China most likely. But again, right at my price point.

Fortunately, the assembly instructions had been so faithfully translated from the original Japanese that anyone with a PhD in engineering could put this stuff together. By the time I was finished, I could curse fluently in several languages.

We officed with Sandy for a year or two. Then I got a call one weekend at home from the building landlord. "Come get your stuff, I'm locking you out."

Again with that! We had been paying Sandy, but Sandy was not paying the landlord. This time, no more subletting. I entered into a lease with the office building owner for space in the basement of the building. We remained in the lower level for the next 20 years.

While our accommodations may have been humble, the address was on a prestigious thoroughfare. That address helped put me on the map.

As I write this, Decker Properties is developing a suburban apartment complex of over 200 units. It is a team effort and there are nearly 50 of us now. It's like nothing we have ever done before, so I find myself learning still. Funny, but South Town Bank has the financing on this one too.

I have always enjoyed my job, if you would call it that. For me, it has been more like a cause. Whatever success I have, I know a big part of it stems from the accumulated undeserved kindness of near strangers.

Do not neglect to show hospitality to strangers, for thereby some have entertained angels unawares.

—Hebrews 13:2

"

"The secret of success is
to be ready when your
opportunity comes."
—Benjamin Disraeli

"

7

WHAT TO SAY WHEN YOU MEET THE MAYOR

For most of my real estate career, Tom Barrett has been among the most influential politicians where I live in southeastern Wisconsin. Mr. Barrett represented the Wisconsin 5th congressional district from 1993 to 2003. In 2004, Mr. Barrett was elected mayor of Milwaukee. Barrett would continue in that capacity until becoming the longest current serving mayor of one of the largest 50 cities in the US. This 18-year mayoral reign ended only when Barrett was named ambassador to Luxembourg in 2022.

There were additional campaigns for governor of Wisconsin that didn't work out. There was a brief time between the end of his congressional career before winning election to mayor of Milwaukee when Tom Barrett served in private law practice. That's when I had the opportunity to meet Mr. Barrett.

I was conducting business in a swank downtown office building in Milwaukee when, my business completed, I boarded the elevator alone to return to my car in the underground garage. The elevator descended only a few floors when the car stopped and in walked the great man himself, Tom Barrett.

A terrific chance opportunity had presented itself. Immediately my mind began to spin about what I might say to this influential man. Hitting upon my answer, I squared my jaw, looked him straight in the eye, and I said to him, "don't I know you from somewhere?"

Other greetings that were rejected:

1. Hi, my name's Dave, how do you like me so far?
2. Is my fly open?
3. Sorry for drooling on your shoe.

Sometimes you swing, and sometimes you miss. When you miss, better to laugh it off. The best jokes are the ones told on yourself. For the record, the current mayor of Milwaukee is Cavalier Johnson. He used to rent an apartment from me.

Let your speech always be gracious, seasoned with salt, so that you may know how you ought to answer each person.   —Colossians 4:6 ESV

SECTION 2

SUCCESS SECRETS

"

"The secret of success is
to do the common things
uncommonly well."
—John D. Rockefeller Jr.

"

8

THE SECRET TO SUCCESS
IN BUSINESS

Congratulations! You've just thought of the next big whiz-bang gizmo. Everyone is going to want one.

Just one thing: where are you going to manufacture that? Should you outsource to Asia? They don't always honor intellectual property the way we do. Maybe you'd better go domestic.

You'll need to locate and equip a factory. Then there's the hiring and training of a workforce to run that factory. If you choose to outsource, will the resulting loss of control compromise your trade secrets and still deliver the quality you want?

You'll need to raise capital. Don't forget about patent protection. Make sure you're properly insured.

Once the factory is up and running, you'll need to meet payroll, pay vendors, ship products in full and on time, and then bill customers. Not all your customers will pay on time, so before long, you will be immersed in receivables management.

Before there can be any customers, there has to be a salesforce. That's likely to be just you in the beginning, but as this thing takes off, you'll need to find and train this unique bunch of vital contributors.

This process above is hardly comprehensive. But it begins to give you a glimpse of what is involved with bringing a new idea to market, even a great idea. Fail at any one of these challenges, and your product idea is likely to become just another fishing story.

That's why the first secret to success in business is the excellent execution of mundane details. There is a second secret that will come in a moment.

The Excellent Execution of Mundane Details

In fact, you can skip the trouble of trying to dream up the next new thing. Succeeding at that is incredibly hard and unlikely. Even so, being able to execute mundane details with excellence is more valuable.

It means that any business you should choose to run can be a runaway success. Yes, location and timing will still be important. Many businesses that have potential never achieve liftoffoff because they are undercapitalized. But even location, timing and financing fit into the realm of mundane details!

Some examples will be illuminating.

Consider Chick-fil-A versus McDonalds:

Chick Fil A	McDonald's
$8.6 Million in annual sales per store[1]	$3 Million in annual sales per store[2]
Open six days a week	Open seven days a week
My order is associated with my name	My order is associated with a number
Staff is enthusiastic	Staff is apathetic
Staff most likely to say: My pleasure!	Staff most likely to say: Have a good one
Chicken sandwich is an industry leader	Chicken sandwich is an afterthought
Waffle fries are always excellent and hot	French fries are excellent, but sometimes cold

Obviously, much of this is subjective. These are two competitors in the same industry, often located in proximity to each other. But what's not subjective are store sales.

In the apartment business, we rise or fall on things like whether the bushes are trimmed, the grass cut and the clippings blown off the walkways and parking lots, the hallways cleaned, weeds removed, litter and pet waste cleaned up, and so on. If these aren't mundane details, I don't know what is.

None of these things are hard to do. But if that's true, then why are many landlords doing such a crummy job? In my experience, poorly maintained landscaping, grubby hallways, and overall poor maintenance and care are commonplace. I'm not complaining, I'm grateful that our competitors are making it easier for us to look good.

I'm always after our staff emphasizing the standard we're trying to achieve with every apartment we turn over to a new resident is new construction. The paint has to be fresh and the carpets cleaned or replaced. Appliances need to be cleaned as if they were new out of the box. Bathrooms need to sparkle. Every cabinet and drawer needs to be inspected and cleaned.

And as if that weren't enough, getting a unit clean and ready for move-in and keeping it ready is another heavy lift. Often in winter, floors can be tracked up from wet shoes. In new construction, there is so much dust still settling that a brand-new apartment that isn't cleaned 24-48 hours before delivery is likely to have a fine coating of dust. The only remedy is to clean and keep cleaning and check and recheck the apartments before they're turned over.

The second secret to success in business is a commitment to continuous improvement.

Commit to Continuous Improvement

Decker Properties has been around for nearly 40 years. I think we're doing great, but I know better than to think that we've arrived. It's embarrassing to think about how we used to do some things. In the beginning, I can remember outfitting apartments with used appliances and deliberately avoiding frills that I perceived troublesome and prone to failure, like automatic defrost!

We used to fill out preprinted leases by hand and then meet with the new resident for signing. We felt compelled to explain the lease in these meetings, and the appointment would last half an hour. Our staff would have to remember which apartments included which utilities and other details subject to human error.

As technology evolved, we began scanning in the paper lease to produce an electronic document that we would email to prospective residents. But this was hardly an improvement. Our residents would have to print out the lease, sign it, and then scan and email it back to us. Often, residents owned only a smartphone and didn't have convenient access to a printer. Our lease requires multiple signatures and initials in several different places in the lease. A new resident often overlooked a required signature or initial.

Once, a single lease had to be printed three times: First by us to email to the resident. Then, the resident would print it a second time to sign it. Upon returning it to us, we would print the lease out for the third time, manually sign and then scan the completed document yet again to email to the resident. Then, we would file the paper copy. Every step was prone to human error or misfiling.

Today, our leases are entirely electronic and produced by computer at the click of a button. The lease is distributed electronically for electronic signature. The document will not allow the user to proceed until all required signatures and initials are completed. The details of who is responsible for utilities are automatically programmed into the electronic document. All parties to the lease can sign at the click of a button. The document is never printed out and is filed electronically. The time and inconvenience saved are massive.

There are other electronic productivity improvements as well.

Instead of opening hundreds of pieces of mail and logging in paper rent checks, tenants make electronic payments and can view their ledger and payment history online at any time. These payments are made through a secure portal without cost to our residents. There is no more speculation about payments being lost or delayed in the mail. This also eliminates the previously frequent questions from residents checking to see if payments were received or inquiring about their balance.

In fact, residents increasingly expect this level of customer service and convenience in signing leases and renewals and submitting payments. Residents expect to have information, such as payment history and rental agreements, readily accessible at their convenience.

Adopting various technologies has allowed us to eliminate rote processes that can be done by machine so we can pay more attention to those details that can only be executed by people.

Our standards are ever evolving as well. Excellence today is merely average tomorrow. The days of used manual defrost refrigerators are long gone. As mentioned earlier, we're striving to deliver an apartment that looks like new construction. And even new construction amenities are a standard that is always rising.

I attend the parade of homes in my area annually to keep abreast of design changes and trends in housing. I am always sure to check out the most expensive, luxurious homes with the finest features. Then, we brainstorm how we can recreate this million-dollar experience in our new construction apartments. Lately, that has meant the inclusion of walk-in tile showers in our apartments with two full baths and attached three-car garages prewired for electric vehicles.

We particularly gravitate toward changes that are not easy to copy. Warren Buffett would call this building a mote. We were early adopters of laminate flooring and then luxury vinyl plank flooring that both look like hardwood floors but are affordable and, at least in the vinyl plank version, impervious to water and spills. The problem is that anyone can copy this, and everyone has.

A better example is our walk-in showers, which feature heated tile floors. These showers require a footprint that is larger than a conventional bathtub. You can certainly incorporate them in your new construction plans but once the building is built, if you didn't install the walk-in shower, it's game over—you can likely never retrofit one in.

Most apartments are about as interesting and unique as a set of identical twins at an undertaker's convention. New construction apartments often rent well because nothing sells like new. But what about 20 years from now? Were you forward-thinking enough to anticipate what the market would want even decades into the future?

The first apartments I developed in 1997 were on a golf course in Fond du Lac, Wisconsin. When the Fairways were first built, I would like to think they were the best apartments in town. Of course, that's subjective. But more objectively, they were the most expensive apartments in town. But what about today? Thanks to our commitment to maintain and even reposition and redevelop the property through time, the Fairways remains one of the most expensive rental housing choices in this small town.

This chapter is titled 'The Secret to Success in Business, ' as if there were only one secret. Already, I've snuck in a second one about the need for continuous improvement! But the most important point of all is this: Success is not the exclusive territory of creative genius. Success does not require dreaming up the next new thing. Success flows from continuous improvement, and the excellent execution of mundane details means that success is within the grasp of just about anyone.

"Do you see a man skillfull in his work? He will stand before kings; he will not stand before obscure men."
—Proverbs 22:29 ESV

"God never said that the
journey would be easy, but
He did say that the arrival
would be worthwhile."
—Max Lucado

9

WHAT TO SAY AT THE GRADUATION – THE MASTER KEY TO SUCCESS

Congratulations graduate! I'm so excited for you. There has never been a better time to launch out into the world. Despite what you may have heard, you live in a country and at a place in time that has never been more free and more fair. The possibilities abound.

What kernel of truth can I share with you to accelerate your way and sharpen your trajectory? Sooner than you realize, more than likely, you will be working full time, married, and have kids of your own. Sharing insight into how to successfully navigate even one of these areas would keep us here until Tuesday.

And yet, what if there was one secret, one strategy, one tactic that, if you learned it, employed it, and lived it, would help you to triumph in all three? Graduate, I submit to you, there is just such a secret. Not only am I going to share it with you, I'm going to prove to you it's true. I'm going to share with you the Master Key to Success.

But be careful. This is no get-rich-quick scheme. The Master Key to Success is easily understood but harder to implement. It's not something you can do occasionally, and expect it to work. It's a way of life. It's like flossing your teeth. To get any benefit, you have to be consistent. It requires us to set aside our human nature and go against everything that comes naturally. I said it would work. I didn't say it would be easy.

Graduate, the Master Key to Success is putting God first.

Putting God First

The order of things is God first, others second, and you last. Put yourself last, and you'll finish first. It sounds counter-intuitive, but it's not even my idea. It's God's idea. Matthew 20:16 ESV says, "So the last will be first, and the first last." This verse comes from the Parable of the Workers in the Vineyard. Various workers showed up at different times of the day, yet the employer paid them all a fair day's wage. The workers who showed up at the beginning of the day were grumbling over the good deal their coworkers got. In other words, the first workers were inwardly focused. They could have rejoiced over the bonus their peers got, but instead, they complained. The choice was theirs to make.

I suspect many hearing this will be disappointed. It's not hard to imagine circumstances from the near future—you may have one of those entry-level jobs with not much glamor, living paycheck to paycheck. You're newly married and have babies at home—you're plenty busy. Then, someone like me comes along and tells you to serve God, too. It's just another load of bricks on the camel's back.

But that's seeing it the wrong way.

Jesus said in Matthew 11:28 ESV, "Come to me, all who labor and are heavy laden, and I will give you rest." Yes, serving God is an additional responsibility. But if you take it on and live the way God wants you to, everything else will go easier for you.

The Promises of God

Let's not misunderstand. God doesn't promise that if you live a godly life, everything will go well for you. In fact, there are warnings about the opposite. In Matthew 6:24 ESV, Jesus said, "If anyone would come after me, let him deny himself and take up his cross and follow me." The cross wasn't a piece of jewelry; it was an instrument of execution designed to torture and humiliate. Jesus is instructing us to deny ourselves, just as mentioned earlier.

2 Timothy 3:12 ESV says, "Indeed, all who desire to live a godly life in Christ Jesus will be persecuted." There may still be health problems, accidents, and other tragedies beyond our control. And none of that even qualifies as persecution. Persecution is when you get passed over for a promotion just because you're a Christian or other suffering specific to your faith.

Despite these maladies, God promises to be with you and guide you and ultimately bless you, but perhaps not in the way you expected.

But I'm burdening you with the folly of my opinions. Let's hear what God says about this:

> This Book of the Law shall not depart from your mouth, but you shall meditate on it day and night so that you may be careful to do according to all that is written in it. For then you will make your way prosperous, and then you will have good success.   —Joshua 1:8 ESV

> "But seek first the kingdom of God and his righteousness, and all these things will be added to you."
> —Matthew 6:33 ESV

> Trust in the Lord with all your heart, and do not lean on your own understanding. ⁶ In all your ways acknowledge him, and he will make straight your paths.
> —Proverbs 3:5-6 ESV

Putting God First in Marriage

By now, you've probably been to a few weddings, so you know how this works. Everyone gets dressed up in their finest. Hair and makeup are perfect, and I'm just talking about the men. The ladies have taken it to another level entirely. There's quite a celebration. Then, in the middle of all the fun, they talk about, "for better or for worse, in sickness and in health, for richer or for poorer...."

God is even more blunt:

But if you do marry, you have not sinned; and if a virgin marries, she has not sinned. But those who marry will face many troubles in this life, and I want to spare you this.   —1 Corinthians 7:28 NIV

That's a scripture you don't often hear quoted during the ceremony!

But often, once the Romeo and Juliet chapter is over and life sets in, things can go sideways. Sometimes, perhaps inadvertently or without intention, one person in the marriage acts in a way that is unloving or disrespectful. Certainly, good communication is an antidote to this problem. However, if the pattern continues, the person on the receiving end of thoughtlessness can begin to lose patience. Maybe the day comes when the aggrieved party thinks or says, "Based on what you've been doing to me, I'm not doing anything for you."

What started as something inadvertent can cross over into premeditation and deliberation. If a way isn't found to stop this trend, two people who promised to love each other forever will be in a contest to see who can hurt the other the most.

Putting God first can be the answer. The disrespect and unloving behaviors are still there. But instead of reacting, the one on the receiving end decides to honor God through marriage. The injured party continues to respond with love and respect, not because the spouse is deserving but because God is deserving. If the transgressor still maintains a shard of decency, they will eventually come around and respond properly.

That's not to say the injured party should suffer in silence. Disappointment should be communicated in a respectful way, being mindful of the timing. Even voicing dissatisfaction can come from a heart of love and respect in a God-honoring fashion.

Marriage Is 50-50?

Have you heard that marriage is supposed to be 50-50? Graduate, that's terrible advice! With this expectation, you will almost certainly be disappointed. We tend to overvalue our own contributions and underappreciate the things done for us. Go into marriage assuming it's going to be 100-0. Don't go into marriage in anticipation of what you'll get out of it, but what you'll put into it.

Is 50-50 what you want? There is one time that you can be sure that your marriage will be 50-50—in divorce court. Graduate, love is grand. Divorce is $100 grand!

Career

What about your career? Imagine two newlywed couples like before—newlywed, living hand to mouth, and babies besides. One couple is moral and upright, but they don't have God in their lives. The second couple is not perfect, but they're doing their best to live for God. The moral couple goes to work. But they have those entry-level jobs where sometimes you work hard all day, but no one seems to notice or care. The worker gets home at the end of the day, and the spouse says, "How was your day, honey?" The worker responds, "I did my best today, but it's as if I'm invisible."

The Christian couple has similar circumstances. They go to work and do their best, but they labor in anonymity. At the end of the day, the spouse says, "How was your day, honey? And the worker responds, "It was a great day today; it was just me and the Lord today."

For God's Eyes Only

Matthew 6:1-2 ESV says this: "Beware of practicing your righteousness before other people in order to be seen by them, for then you will have no reward from your Father who is in heaven. ² "Thus when you give to the needy, sound no trumpet before you, as the hypocrites do in the synagogues and in the streets, that they may be praised by others. Truly, I say to you, they have received their reward.

The idea continues in Matthew 6:5 ESV: "And when you pray, you must not be like the hypocrites, for they love to stand and pray in the synagogues and at the street corners, that they may be seen by others. Truly, I say to you, they have received their reward.

Consider Colossians 3:23 ESV: Whatever you do, work heartily, as for the Lord and not for men.

Clearly, God is telling us what is done for his eyes only is something special. Doing good when God is the only witness is an opportunity for worship without stepping inside a church.

Check you motives—they have to be pure, extended without the thought or expectation of gain.

Finally, your labors may not be as secret as you think.

You're Not As Anonymous As You Think

We live in a surveillance state and a world of big data. At my company, we manage 1,700 apartments. They're scattered all over Wisconsin. I get to some of these buildings only a few times per year and only meet with the workers there just as often. But I've always known how everyone is doing.

Maintenance requests come in all the time, usually in the form of an electronic record. The requests are disseminated automatically to the appropriate maintenance staff for attention. As the requests are cleared, a database of completed service records accumulates. Those records are searchable electronically. In a few clicks, it's possible to know how many requests a worker cleared, when they were cleared, how they were cleared, and if there were any callbacks for something not done right the first time.

Yet I'm an old-school guy—I've never searched that database. I've been an employer for over 30 years. For most of that time, this kind of data wasn't available. But if you're immersed in your business, you just know how your staff are doing. Your employer may not know the details of any given day, but chances are they have a firm grasp of the big picture.

If you show up on time, ready to work, and have a great attitude, you've just distinguished yourself from 90% of the workforce. Make it even better by avoiding the office gossip.

Don't Grumble About Your Boss or Employer

Once you land your first full-time job, or even before, you'll encounter grumbling about the boss or the company. Don't participate. Every person in a position of authority is there with the full knowledge and consent of God.

Consider Romans 13:1-2 ESV: Let every person be subject to the governing authorities. For there is no authority except from God, and those that exist have been instituted by God. [2] Therefore whoever resists the authorities resists what God has appointed, and those who resist will incur judgment.

This truth can be vexing. It applies not only to your boss but even to political leaders. How is it that God allows such scoundrels to get elected or reach high places of authority?

In ancient times, the Israelites had no earthly king and were governed instead by judges, and God spoke to the people through prophets. Yet the Israelites desired an earthly king like other nations:

Then all the elders of Israel gathered together and came to [the prophet] Samuel at Ramah [5] and said to him, "Behold, you are old, and your sons do not walk in your ways. Now appoint for us a king to judge us like all the nations."   —1 Samuel 8:4-5 ESV

This is the temptation all of us experience, both as individuals and as a nation. The way of the world seems appealing. The consequences, if any, seem far off. The Bible says sin can be pleasurable for a season (Hebrews 11:25).

But in this instance, God warns the Israelites of their folly. In 1 Samual 8:10-18, God cautions that an earthly king will conscript their sons for the army, require the people to work his fields, take their daughters to be housekeepers, confiscate their lands and their harvests, take their best employees and a portion of their livestock, and to top it off; they'll even become his slaves. And when the day comes when the people cry out in their misery caused by this king they chose, God will not answer them.

Did the people listen? No! They demanded a king like the other nations. And the Lord said to Samuel, "Obey their voice and make them a king...." 1 Samuel 8:22 ESV

Whether a nation or an individual, God allows people to pursue their first love, be that God or the world. That's how scoundrels get elected and promoted.

We are instructed by God not to grumble:

Do all things without grumbling or disputing, [15] that you may be blameless and innocent, children of God without blemish in the midst of a crooked and twisted generation, among whom you shine as lights in the world. —Philippians 2:14-15 ESV

Complying with Authority

The Bible says there is nothing new under the sun (Ecclesiastes 1:9). People today grumble about paying taxes to a wasteful government pursuing objectionable policies. Our ancestors had the same problem. In Bible times, the Jewish leaders were trying to trick Jesus about paying taxes to a government considered corrupt and oppressive. Jesus famously said to them:

> "Show me the coin for the tax." And they brought him a denarius.[20] And Jesus said to them, "Whose likeness and inscription is this?" [21] They said, "Caesar's." Then he said to them, "Therefore render to Caesar the things that are Caesar's, and to God the things that are God's."
>
> —Matthew 22:19–21

Context is important. The Roman government was indeed corrupt and oppressive. It was far worse than anything we know today. Odds are your boss is far gentler than any Roman master. We have no reason to grumble.

Grumbling reflects a lack of trust in God's provision, plan, or presence. That's not to say that you can't take legitimate complaints to the boss so long as they are respectfully presented and thoughtfully timed. And if things are really bad, get another job. You're not required to be a doormat.

Not grumbling is a good start, but consider your employer with fresh eyes—as the only customer of your very small business.

An Employee is an Entrepreneur with One Customer

Have you heard that the customer is king? There might be something to that. If you're an employee working for an employer, then you are like a small business person with just one customer! You had better make sure your only customer is treated well. It's OK if your employer is getting the better end of the deal. And while you're working hard, it won't hurt if there's a little sunshine emanating from your face. Be diligent and have a good attitude. Make your boss look good. Take problems off his or her plate. Help out without being asked.

What About the Employer?

The preceding advice must sound tremendously self-serving since I am an employer. I've learned a thing or two about treating customers like kings. My customers are the tenants living in my apartments. If I want them to be treated well, I better treat the employees like they are royalty. Good employees are golden. They deserve respect and understanding. Sometimes, it feels like they get paid like gold is free!

There Are No Bargains in Wages

In business, there are entire libraries of management books dedicated to the goal of trying to get the workforce to do a better job and work harder without paying them more. I'm not saying those books don't have good ideas, but an employer that pays well has an advantage.

In sports, there are salary caps. It keeps the game competitive, and the policy sure seems effective. At the start of every season, many fans are hopeful that this could be the championship year. It's rare for one team to dominate for a long time. Even individual games are likely to be see-saw battles decided in the closing minutes, keeping fans at the edge of their seats all the way.

Fortunately, businesses don't have these artificial constraints. Instead, you're free to recruit the best talent you can, pay them well, treat them with respect, give them the flexibility to pursue their other interests and obligations, and then stomp all over the competition.

Recently, I had lunch with a landlord friend of mine. During the meal, he lamented the difficulty he was having in filling maintenance positions. Even before I asked, I knew what the problem was going to be. "How much are you paying your best guy," I inquired. He mentioned a rate that was about 20% less than what I was paying our least skilled employee.

The question is not who you would rather work for; it's where you would rather live. Our tenant prospects don't get to see the details of our payroll, but they do see the well-manicured grounds, the helpful staff, the pristine common areas, and the like-new apartments.

Let's complete this section with Colossians 4:1 ESV: Masters, treat your bondservants justly and fairly, knowing that you also have a Master in heaven.

Zero Sum Thinking

Some think that if the employees are paid more, the employer must receive less. This is zero-sum thinking. If the employees are paid well and treated with kindness and respect, the employees will do a great job, the customers will be pleased, the business will grow, and the employer will make more than ever.

Business is important. But never take your eyes off the prize—our children.

Kids

What about raising kids? That's about the hardest job there is, just ask your parents. You don't have to worry about putting a newborn first. They'll demand that from you. Then, as they get a little older, it gets more complicated. Have you heard about spending quality time with your children? Sounds like an excuse from someone not spending quantity time with their children. Kids require both.

You can't fake it with your kids. They will know where your priorities lie. You can continue with your hobbies and interests. Just make sure you take your kids along. Turn off your phone and talk to them. You never talk down to your kids. Talk up to them. Go ahead and have conversations on adult topics using words they might not understand yet. They'll stop you for clarification. Don't talk to them like the kids they are now; speak to them like the adults they will become.

Give them opportunities to participate in adult activities like loading the dishwasher or doing laundry. Notice I didn't say chores. When they're very young, it's like getting to play adult. Yes, the dishes might get broken, and the laundry may come out with everything pink. They've got more of that stuff at Walmart.

Tell your kids what they need to know long before the knowledge is needed. Conversations about the responsibilities of driving can take place at 14. By 16, it's too late. I don't know when conversations start about birds and bees, but earlier than you think!

Proving the Master Key to Success

God first, others second, you last. It's the master key to success. I promised I would prove it to you. Let's do that.

Who is the most important person in history? Who is better known than anyone else? It's a tricky question. Some people can command tremendous attention for a brief time, but the most famous person of all time is Jesus Christ.

Jesus lived 2000 years ago, but people still assemble weekly to learn more about him. He is known all over. Every December 25th, the world stops to remember his birthday.

When Jesus knew he would soon be crucified, he called his team together for one last strategic planning session. These 12 men soon would be charged with carrying the mantle of leadership forward without him. Wanting to impart one last management lesson, Jesus convened a final meal. Before they ate, he got down on his knees and washed their feet. Then Jesus went to the cross and died for the sins of the world. Talk about putting others first! That was no benefit to Jesus but a benefit to every believer to the present day.

Nothing will give you a better chance at success than the Master Key to Success. But I caution you. Nothing works all the time, every time. There can be hard, difficult moments.

It's easy to be Christ-like when things are going well. It's not until the cross draws near that we find out what Christianity is all about. I call those seasons of the cross.

Seasons of the Cross

I've had more than a few of those. There was a young man I knew that didn't get much of a chance in life. His father was an alcoholic. Dad committed suicide when the boy was young. By the time this boy was a young man in his early 30s, he was living at home with his mom, with no job, no money, no car, and not much hope.

That's when I got involved. I set this young man up in a nice apartment—one of mine —and gave him a job working for me, making more money than he ever had in his life. I had him train with one of our best workers. I loaned him some money to get his driver's license out of hock.

He didn't have a car, so I gave him one of mine. I don't mean I loaned him a car; I transferred the title.

I met some material needs, but there were some needs of the soul that went unmet. He was an angry young man. He was difficult to work with and didn't represent us well with our customers. I called him into my office one day—he didn't know why—but it was to talk about his anger. We didn't make it very far in the conversation before he got mad and stomped out the door. Not much later, he got mad and quit. Shortly after that, I learned he had been stealing from me the entire time he had been working for us.

Hard, bitter things.

Seasons of Victory

You've heard about when it doesn't work; let's talk about when it does. I've only been married one time. I don't have the perfect marriage—does anyone? But I know my wife is one of the many ways God has chosen to bless me. To the extent my marriage isn't better, it's only because I often fail to follow my own advice. Regardless of the state of my marriage, I know how and when it's going to end—when death do us part. I thank God for my wife.

What about my career? My business was successful enough that I got to come here today to share in your graduation. I even got to write a book about that success.

But my favorite accomplishment is my kids. My wife gets most of the credit for that. She was a stay-at-home mom and a homeschool educator.

I have a son and a daughter. There was never a time I had to talk to my daughter about something she was wearing being too short or too tight. There was never a time when there were loud arguments, slamming doors, or a disgruntled teenager shut away in a bedroom. I never had to worry about my kids breaking curfew. They never even had a curfew. My daughter just graduated from a Christian university with an education degree and will soon be teaching in a Christian school.

Tragically, my son is a money-grubbing capitalist, just like his father. He started trading stocks at 15 and has done amazingly well. He has taken to weightlifting and physical fitness and is planning on being a personal trainer and opening his own gym. He looks like someone who should be a personal trainer. They are two of the most decent, honorable people I know.

In all, my life has been an embarrassment of riches. Had the Lord come to me when I was young and offered me anything I wanted, I wouldn't have been smart enough to ask for all that I have.

Put God first, others second. Put yourself last, and you'll finish first. It's the Master Key to Success. Try it, live it, and I'll see you at the top. Congratulations, and God bless you.

"The greatest among you shall be your servent. Whoever exalts himself will be humbled, and whoever humbles himself will be exalted."   —Matthew 23:11-12 ESV

"I find that the harder I work,

the more luck I seem

to have."

—Thomas Jefferson

10

THE BEST COMPANY TO WORK FOR IN AMERICA

This will be the shortest chapter in this book because, of course the answer is Decker Properties, Inc! However, if you don't live in Wisconsin, perhaps the topic warrants further examination.

Every year, magazines and other publications spill considerable ink (or consume numerous bytes), anointing the best companies to work for. I'm skeptical. Even if these companies are as wonderful as reported, that won't help if your boss at Wonderful Company is a jerk. Even if your supervisor is inspiring, you can still get stuck in the wrong job, have the wrong commute, or be living in a part of the country you hate. Perhaps determining the best company to work for in America is akin to deciding which flavor of aspirin is best when you're determined to continue hitting yourself in the head with a hammer. The best company to work for in America is your own.

Tired of having to put up with a bunch of ingrates? Once you're in control, office politics and difficult supervisors and coworkers are a thing of the past. Tired of making the company rich? Now is the time to make some bank. Need flexibility for childcare or other obligations? Here it is. Ready to exercise your passions? Now you can. Tired of creative constraints? Blast off to the moon in your own rocket ship. Is reporting to the office encroaching on your travel dreams when you know you could do this gig on the road? Pack your bags. Being held back from exploring new skills or cultivating fresh knowledge? Here's your chance to craft your own PhD. Bored with mundane tasks? Outsource those and focus on what you do best. Stuck in an undesirable routine? Blaze your own trail where every day is new.

According to Inc.com, 63% of 20-somethings want to start their own business. Until that day comes, they are probably employees. And there's only one kind of employee that you want to be. An employee is an entrepreneur with a single customer.

An Employee Is an Entrepreneur with One Customer

If you are 100% dependent on one customer to keep your enterprise afloat, you had better treat that customer well. Employers are desperate for workers who think like owners. Thinking like an owner means that you take the initiative to solve problems if you know the solution, even if the challenge doesn't immediately impact you.

Look, act, and live the part. Years ago, I was closing a real estate transaction, selling a property for an elderly, conservative client. The closing was held at a local title company on a Friday near the end of a month. Our file wasn't ready, so we had to wait a considerable time in the lobby. While waiting, numerous title company personnel scurried through the lobby, some unprofessionally dressed. The end of a week at the end of a month can be a time of peak activity for title companies. That our file wasn't ready might have been acceptable by itself, but the combination of the delay with the inappropriate attire embarrassed me in front of my client. I never used that title company again.

We all make mistakes, and there will be moments when our work product just isn't sharp. But we can always look sharp. This will probably draw laughs from my coworkers at Decker Properties because I'm often in shorts and sandals all summer long. But we don't have frequent customer contact. Furthermore, whether good or bad, my reputation is established and well-known. How I dress now isn't going to fool anyone!

But it wasn't always that way. I remember years ago, when I was involved as a broker in another real estate transaction, there was an attorney giving me a hard time. He wasn't returning my calls and on the rare occasion when I was able to talk to him, I sensed a condescending attitude. Time to go pay Mr. Attorney a visit. I typically wore a suit back in those days anyway, so for this visit, I was sure to put on my best suit with the athletic cut, the freshly pressed dress shirt, and a power tie. All I needed to do was drop off a file, so I figured I didn't need an appointment. I went to his office, introduced myself to the receptionist and proceeded to wait. It wasn't long before Mr. Attorney emerged from his edifice. Where he had hair, it was curly and looking windblown. He had a bit of a pot belly, and his suit jacket was off. His shirt was short-sleeved and his tie was at half-mast. It didn't hurt that I was several inches taller.

"Nice to meet you, Mr. Attorney. Dave Decker, with Decker Properties. I just wanted to drop off this file and make sure it gets to you," was about all I said before I left. But it was enough. From that point on there were no further problems with returned calls or conversing as anything other than equals.

Particularly when I was younger, I was very protective of the image I portrayed, whether that image was defined by how I dressed or the work product I was producing. I knew I was an unknown and would likely get only one chance to make a good impression. Anything associated with me had to be top notch. I still feel that way about the way our apartments are maintained and how we conduct business.

It's been a few years now, but I used to get soaked in sweat as I visited properties and collected litter, broke down abandoned furniture and tossed it in the dumpster and made other tweaks and adjustments as necessary to elevate that property as best I could in as little time as I had available. It wasn't necessarily my plan to have my associates see me doing this, but often they did and setting that example has been invaluable. I don't excuse myself from the humblest of work, and hopefully, the rest of the team doesn't either. We all just do what we can while we can the best we can whenever we can.

This is what your single-customer employer should see in you. Today, we have updates to cliches about doing half a job. It used to be called mailing it in. Now it's quiet quitting, grumpy staying, bare minimum Mondays, lazy girl jobs, and others. Just understand who the ultimate loser is in this equation and it's not the employer. If you're so dissatisfied with your job that you're just faking it, do yourself a favor and find something else you can throw yourself into body and soul.

I know not all work is glamorous. But I want an excellent outcome for my enterprise. If that means in this moment, I need to pick up cigarette butts, then that's what I'll be doing. I'm proud of what we've accomplished as a team and the culture that has evolved while doing it.

Engaging the world like an entrepreneur is an approach that you should always be taking, even if you never start your own business. And here's a secret that few people would dare tell you. Perhaps starting your own business is not the right move for you. Let's look at why.

The Perils of Owning Your Own Business

The Covid 19 pandemic resulted in a flourishing of new businesses as laid-off employees became entrepreneurs. In 2022, approximately five million new businesses were formed, nearly twice the pre-pandemic norm.

I started my own company in 1990. I was 27. There are about 50 of us now, and I have no plans to slow down. Working for someone else seems unimaginable. And yet not everyone has such a rosy experience. That's why I want to share ten land-mines entrepreneurs often fail to avoid.

1. Only half of all startups survive five years according to the Bureau of Labor Statistics. This is not to suggest that half of all businesses fail. Some might get bought out by other businesses or merely undergo a name change.

Regardless, the probability of long-term survival is perilous.

2. Even businesses that "survive the five" may not be thriving. Perhaps the business owner would have been better off financially had they remained an employee.

3. Some entrepreneurs go the franchise route. However, franchisors can dictate products, methods and territory. The franchisee may have little more autonomy than a corporate middle manager.

4. Some entrepreneurs raise venture capital to start their businesses. This means instead of answering to a boss, you answer to investors.

5. Some entrepreneurs go into business with partners. Having a business partner is akin to having a marriage partner and half of all marriages fail. Business partnerships do too.

6. Being in business for yourself can be isolating. For introverts like me, that's no problem. But if comradery or collaboration is your thing, beware of the isolation that can come with starting your own business.

7. Starting a new business can be an all-consuming endeavor. This is probably not going to be a 9-5 gig. What about work-life balance? Is your spouse fully onboard and working with you shoulder to shoulder? Or are they getting dragged along on a ride they never wanted? And what about the kids? Can they get involved, or are you going to become a stranger to them? Even friends and extended family can feel left out, victims of your new

enterprise. Go back to number six and reconsider the possibility of isolation with fresh eyes.

8. You could go broke. If you're an employee and you guess wrong or do a lousy job, you could get fired. However, if you own the business and make too many mistakes, you could take your entire financial life down with the ship.

9. You are going to make mistakes. When you were an employee and made a mistake, chances are the company ate that. You'll be eating your own mistakes from now on. Once you have employees of your own, you'll be eating their mistakes too.

10. It costs more than you thought. I'll never forget my new office when I first started. I was surrounded by second-hand equipment and assembled yourself office furniture comprised of pictures of wood over particle board. It all cost around $10,000, and that was in 1990.

Whether you start your own business someday or not give thought to Colossians 3:23-24 ESV:

Whatever you do, work heartily, as for the Lord and not for men, [24] knowing that from the Lord you will receive the inheritance as your reward.

"I'm not buying a house for investment—I'm buying a place to live. Investments come later."

—Barbara Corcoran

11

THE WORST INVESTMENT YOU'LL EVER MAKE

What do you suppose the worst investment you could ever make would be? Vintage comic books? Old beer can collections? Belgium tulip bulbs? None of those sound particularly promising, but the worst investment you're ever likely to make is the home you own and live in.

That may sound a little self-serving coming from the guy making his living as a landlord. Let me try another approach that might be a little more palatable: The home you live in is the best consumer purchase you will ever make. But it's still a lousy investment.

Most consumer purchases lose all or nearly all their value immediately upon purchase. Think a bag of groceries or dinner out. For a consumer purchase to retain any value, the item must be nonperishable, and there must be a robust secondary market for the used item. Used cars are a good example, but used cars still lose value over time. That your house stands to increase in value over time sets it apart as the champion among consumer purchases.

Beware that home price appreciation is not guaranteed. A more complete discussion on that topic can be found in my book, *Cash In On the Coming Real Estate Crash,* published in January 2006, about 30 months before real estate markets crashed. But I'll concede that home prices do a good job of keeping pace with inflation most of the time. I'll further concede that you need a place to live, and a single-family home can be a tremendous source of pride, physical security, and comfort.

But it's still a lousy investment.

Owning stocks is a good investment. What's better than owning 100 shares of Microsoft? Owning 1000 shares of Microsoft. In other words, for actual good investments, if a little is good, more is always better.

So if a 2,000-square-foot home is a good investment, a 20,000-square-foot home must be a much better investment. But obviously, for most people, even if they could afford a 20,000-square-foot home, that wouldn't be a good investment. It would be a budget buster of mortgage interest, upkeep, insurance, and property taxes.

The purchase of a home lights the fuse to further financial disaster. A new house needs new furniture doesn't it? And wouldn't the living room just come alive with all-new window treatments? One of the reasons a robust real estate market ordinarily helps the nation recover from recession is the resulting cascade of consumer purchases associated with home acquisition.

The National Association of Realtors is more than happy to report on the economic feasibility of various home improvements, such as a kitchen remodel or bathroom update. Kitchen remodels typically feature a recovery rate of 67%, and bathroom upgrades fetch 71% recovery in 2022. What exactly does a 67% recovery mean? It means an immediate 33% loss! Enjoy your new kitchen; you certainly paid for it.

Want to turn your home into a good investment? Find someone with a home about the same value as yours and sell him your home, buy his and rent from each other. Now that you're a landlord, you're eligible for depreciation benefits. I've been a landlord since I was 23. Real estate investing is the first, last and best chance for average folks like you and me to become financially independent. I love real estate and being a landlord. If you love your home, I'm happy for you. Just don't buy into the illusion that it's a good investment.

Here's a litmus test for whether your home is a good investment: Can you rent your home to a third party and cover the costs of mortgage payments, insurance, taxes and repairs? The chances are if you can answer yes to this question, it's because your mortgage balance is very low relative to your home's value. If you're getting the equivalent of a $2,000 annual cash flow on a home equity position of $300,000, that's a lousy rate of return on your equity. Typically, a small, modest house has the best chance of being rented out at a positive cash flow, as described above. Suburban behemoths are a money pit.

When a House Is a Good Investment

Having pontificated at length about why a single-family home is a poor investment, let me completely frustrate you by talking about why a house might be a reasonable investment choice. The idea that a house is a poor investment assumes that you are going to invest in superior investment vehicles. The two superior opportunities most investors gravitate toward are investment real estate and the stock market.

Obviously, I'm a big believer in real estate investing. Real estate investing is defined by real estate you buy to rent to somebody else, in contrast to a home you live in. While it's a great opportunity, it's not for everyone. Exploring all the nuances of real estate investing is beyond the scope of this book; however, not everyone wants to deal with tenants or appreciates the illiquidity associated with real estate investing.

For those who find real estate investing unappealing, stock markets are usually the next consideration. But there's no easy money here either. Stock market investing is also beyond the scope of this book, but I'll share some key ideas.

Stock market investing can be a real gut check. You have to learn to love the small loss. For example, say you buy a stake in Acme Company. Acme pays a generous dividend, and it seems poised for a bright future. Naturally, as soon as you buy in, the value of Acme declines by 10%. What do you do now?

At a minimum, you have to unemotionally reevaluate your commitment to Acme. Maybe you should sell. This is where loving the small loss comes in. You've just sustained a relatively small loss. If you had $1,000 invested in Acme, you've now got only $900. The good news is that your 10% loss can be recovered if you are able to invest the remaining $900 capital at an 11% annual return. But what happens if you ride Acme all the way down to a 50% loss? Now, your $1,000 is only worth

$500. To restore the $1000, you need to reinvest the remaining $500 at a 100% annual return. A 100% annual return is very hard to achieve.

Knowing all this, you decide to take the small loss of 10%. Whereupon Acme regains the 10%, and you're left fuming. Gut check time.

In short, stock market investing will torture your soul. It is very humbling. It requires you to admit when you are wrong. For those who master these conundrums, there is considerable money to be made. But it's obviously not for everyone.

So, back to our owner-occupied single-family home as an investment vehicle. Maybe you're the type that's handy with tools and has a flair for decorating on a budget. You may be able to increase the value of your home by far more than the cost of the improvements.

Carrying a mortgage is like a forced savings plan. If your mortgage is 6%, accelerating the prepayment of your mortgage (paying it down faster) is a guaranteed 6% return on your cash. A 6% guaranteed rate of return can be hard to beat sometimes.

Is a home a good investment? A lot depends on you and how you manage your situation. Now let's think about How Much to Charge, which is the topic of the next chapter.

"Do not lay up for yourselves treasures on earth, where moth and rust[a] destroy and where thieves break in and steal, [20] but lay up for yourselves treasures in heaven, where neither moth nor rust destroys and where thieves do not break in and steal. [21] For where your treasure is, there your heart will be also." —Matthew 6:19-21 ESV

"Price is what you pay.

Value is what you get."

—Warren Buffett

12

HOW MUCH TO CHARGE

Short answer: more. Raise your prices. Raise them high; raise them now. Don't be embarrassed about making a profit. Sometimes the profit margin you were hoping for disappears into a margin of error. Raise your prices.

If the only thing you bring to the table is the willingness to work for less, then you will always be vulnerable to the competitor that is willing to accept still less. You have unique attributes—now you just need to get paid for having them.

No one likes a price increase. That's where selling comes in. You cannot go into your boss's office demanding a raise, all pumped up from reading a motivational book. You have to justify every penny of your existence. Keep timing in mind. Maybe you are setting new precedents of excellence doing your job, but the company is suffering. You may need to wait to make your case.

Years ago, I was remodeling the balconies of an apartment building. I put the job out to bid with several contractors. The lowest bid was less than half of some of the other bids. I noticed that one of the higher bids had gone into considerable detail, quantifying all the labor hours involved and the materials required, including lumber. I noticed that the cost of lumber alone exceeded the price of the low bid! I checked the lumber prices at a big box hardware store and found this higher estimate to be accurate.

Had I accepted the low bid, that would not have ended well for anyone. I went with the more costly proposal from the contractor who had done a better job of doing his homework and documenting all that was involved to complete the job properly. In other words, the contractor with the higher bid did a better job of selling.

Being thorough and prepared can win the day, but the fear of customer reaction often prevents entrepreneurs and employees from getting what they are worth. I have certainly lived this fear.

Several years ago, I purchased a 40-unit apartment building out of foreclosure. There were 32 vacant apartments. The eight units occupied were all low-income elderly residents on government rent subsidies. The vacant apartments were not going to rent in their present state. Therefore, we embarked upon a massive renovation.

We built new detached garages where none existed before. We did the landscaping over. Common hallways were redecorated. Individual apartments received new kitchens, including appliances, new flooring, and other updates. Every stick of wood was removed and replaced with new doors and trim. The apartments looked like new construction when we were done.

As this work was going on, the eight original elderly residents were home all day to watch. I knew what was going to happen. All eight would want the new stuff, too.

I did not have the budget to renovate all 40 apartments. I was just planning on remodeling the 32 that were vacant. I would remodel the occupied eight later when more funds were available.

Knowing that I needed to stall on remodeling the occupied units, I devised a plan to discourage these elderly tenants from demanding a new apartment. First, the renovations were too extensive to complete while the apartments were occupied. Therefore, the first step to getting a new apartment would involve having to move, if only across the hall.

Second, these elderly, fixed low-income tenants were going to have to pay the new market rent for a new apartment, a 25% increase in rent. Further, they were going to need to increase their security deposit to the same value as the market rent as well. In short, to get a new apartment, these elderly residents had to be willing to move and pay a substantial sum both upfront and each month. I figured none of them would be willing or able to accept this opportunity and I would be spared from having to remodel eight additional apartments.

Did my plan work? It worked beautifully—for the elderly residents. All eight of them took the deal! I had to immediately remodel 40 apartments instead of 32. I had to scramble to find the money to do it. The existing tenants loved their new apartments and all of them continued to live in their new homes until they either died or moved to a nursing facility.

People are willing to pay extra for something that is a bit nicer, even to someone who sounds like a complete Scrooge like me.

I May Be a Scrouge, but at Least I Have Hair

Years ago, a gentleman stopped by my office. He was completely bald. I don't mean that he had a chrome dome; I mean that he had no eyebrows, no eyelashes, no hair whatsoever. When his real estate enterprise unraveled, the stress caused him to lose his hair—all of it.

I had another friend ask me to prepare a broker's price opinion on an apartment building he was having to relinquish to the lender. The technical term is deed in lieu of foreclosure. While touring the apartments together, he mentioned how difficult it was to inform his wife they were also going to be losing their suburban home. I do not want to wind up hairless, homeless, and broke. If I am ashamed about my profits, my shame is only limited to why they are not more.

There is such a thing as a business cycle. There are good times and bad, and I've certainly seen both. For the average person working as an employee, losing your job can be devastating. But another job can be found. For the entrepreneur, failure can mean losing everything.

For the Christian, we need to trust in the Lord for everything all the time. But that doesn't mean that we are excused from making wise choices. Mathew 10:16 ESV says, "Behold, I am sending you out as sheep in the midst of wolves, so be wise as serpents and innocent as doves."

Earning a profit means that you get to survive to see another year, another quarter, another month.

How to Sell a Price Increase

I have a friend who is a consultant. His schedule is brutal—long hours, lots of travel. He has plenty of work, but he has difficulty hiring partners and employees to help with the surplus. Potential helpers cannot grit out the time commitment and travel. If my friend cannot find helpers, that means the competitors can't either. In fact, competition may be sparse because of the demands of schedule and distance. If there were ever a circumstance ripe for a price increase, this would be it.

Start with the least desirable customer that you would be willing to lose. See if you can secure an increase. Continue with the more desirable customers. The conversation with them can include the fact that other customers have accepted the increase.

Whatever you are doing, you should always be the best value, but not the lowest price. Even if you think what you're selling is a commodity, there is still a way to impart unique value.

Nobody understands this better than Clint P., our lumber supplier at a large building supply house. I keep reminding Clint what he is selling really does grow on trees and he needs to get his prices down!

Clint knows that if all he's got to offer is a lower price on a 2x4, that will only win business until a competitor has it for less. Clint is a solutions partner. Whatever conundrum we're facing in the construction world, Clint is often a reservoir of solutions. The general contractor that has helped us build hundreds of apartments is someone I was introduced to by Clint. Many of the subcontractors and tradespeople we use were also referred to us by Clint. Clint has scoured the landscape to find obscure parts we needed even when the final sale value was very small.

Sometimes, being the best value means reminding the customer of all you've been doing for them. Our property management software allows us to keep track of replacements and repairs made by apartment. When it's lease renewal time and a substantial rent increase has to be sold, that resident will get a detailed report on all we've done for them over the last year as a way of justifying the new rate.

A price increase is often the difference between prosperity and just getting by. Often, the cost of completing a job is fixed. A price increase flows right to the bottom line.

Is Your Passion Keeping You in the Poor House?

Entrepreneurs need to be careful that their passion and enthusiasm aren't keeping them in the poor house. Entrepreneurs can be hard workers and not clock watchers. Sometimes, it may be a good idea to measure all the time you put into a job or a sale to see just how much you're making per hour. Prepare to be shocked.

Price increases are hard but necessary. In recent years, operating costs in the apartment business have exploded. Fortunately, rents have gone up too. Rents are increasing faster than incomes, and our tenants are feeling the pinch. Sometimes when our residents receive their increase notice, our leasing agent gets an earful. We've even been threatened with lawsuits.

But typically, the individual stays in their apartment and pays the increase.

Price increases take courage. You may be all alone in proposing an increase. One of our leasing agents was a rock star. She cared for her residents. She helped elderly residents make out checks to pay their bills. She drove others to their doctor's appointments. She was managing market-rate apartments, not senior housing.

If she had one fault, her empathy for our residents made it nearly impossible for her to advocate for a rent increase. Never mind that she was managing the building with the eight elderly aid recipients described earlier. In other words, she had been a witness to residents volunteering for an increase they could have avoided.

One year, I told her I was going to tie her increase in pay to the same increase in rent we would pass along to the residents. She replied, "Then don't give me an increase this year." We still passed along an increase, and she received a wage adjustment as well.

Price Increases Take Courage

Nine years ago, I was building 82 apartments in a smaller community. Sometimes, when the costs of a construction job come back, they are higher than anticipated. That happened to me on this job. I did what I could to reign the costs in, but they were still too high relative to the original assumption about what we would charge for rent. The only way to resolve the problem was to assume a higher rent would be possible.

In this instance, it was more than wishful thinking. I did research to develop rent comparables that would support our construction costs. However, due to the lack of new construction in the immediate vicinity, I had to look farther afield to find these comparable properties. While I was working on this, a broker friend of mine called me to see how I was doing with the development. When I explained my cost problem and the solution—higher rents—he shared his opinion with me: "I don't think you can get those kinds of rents in that community!"

"I sure hope you're wrong," I replied. "I already broke ground!" The development went on to be a success, but sometimes it takes courage.

Years earlier, I owned a small apartment building and passed along a modest rent increase. One resident got mad and moved out. She moved to an apartment complex in the neighboring community. A few years later, I bought that apartment complex too. You can run, but you can't hide!

No one knows what the future holds, but if history is a guide, then it's likely to cost more than anticipated. Surviving the inevitable booms and busts means being vigilant about protecting your profit margins. Therefore, raise your prices. Raise them high; raise them now.

In all toil there is profit, but mere talk tends only to poverty. —Proverbs 14:23 ESV

"We are what we repeatedly

do. Excllence, then, is not

an act, but a habit."

—Will Durant

(paraphrasing Aristotle)

13

HOW TO LOSE 20 POUNDS

This chapter isn't about how to lose weight. That's just an example. This chapter is about developing strategies to win against every hard thing you may encounter. But losing weight is a handy example. Obesity plagues our nation. According to a Center for Disease Control survey from 2021—2023, over 40% of US adults are obese, and 74% of adults are overweight.

It goes without saying that before getting involved in any diet or exercise regimen, get a complete checkup with your doctor—and all the friendly attorneys at Bludgeon and Ruin can just stand down.

For the record, I've lost 20 lbs. and kept it off. Never mind, I should never have gained the weight in the first place. But I work out six mornings per week, and I can get my pants on without the use of power tools, so I feel qualified to pontificate.

How We Got Here

Before we get any further into the details, let's examine how we got where we are now. Whatever your situation, your current circumstances are a direct result of the decisions you have made so far. Said another way, our spiritual condition, quality of our relationships, financial position, level of fitness and every other facet of our lives is a result of the day-to-day decisions made over a lifetime. Often, these decisions are made so frequently that they become habits.

The 21-Day Rule

Perhaps you've heard of the 21-Day Rule. This idea or rule suggests that it takes approximately 21 days to break one habit and replace it with another. Therefore, whether it be a fitness goal, spiritual objective, or financial aspiration, all of them are within three weeks of our grasp. Right?

Let's see if we can gain insight into this idea by applying what we've already learned. From the Apollo Solution, we want to gain an answer quickly. The Apollo Solution is a close cousin to Wisdom—doing the right thing, right now. Of course, one can always cheat by looking this one up on a smartphone. But I challenge you to turn off the technology and try this one on your own. See if you can come up with a Rhetorical Reality Face Punch that stops all other arguments in their tracks.

How about this one—for the 21-Day Rule to be true, every habit has to be equally hard to break, and every person has to be the same. Said another way, all habits are equal and all of us must have equal discipline or lack thereof. In other words, the 21-Day Rule is complete nonsense. For now, know that some habits are much harder to break than others, and even more importantly, the difficulty of breaking habits and establishing new ones varies widely from individual to individual.

Let's begin our journey by inquiring which diet plan is the most effective. An internet search on the words, "best diet plan" returned 10 pages of detail the day I wrote this. In other words, there's no shortage of opinions on how to proceed. But which plan is best?

Here's a secret. I suspect every plan if followed faithfully, will result in losing weight. In this way, every plan is a success strategy. However, we're all familiar with the yo-yo dieting effect of losing and then regaining weight repeatedly. If the weight is regained, the ultimate outcome is failure.

Let's dig a little deeper by considering a specific diet, the Cabbage Soup Diet (CSD). I must admit that I didn't conduct thorough research on the CSD. Just a glance at the plan includes a suggestion that it can help you lose ten pounds in a single week, so perhaps it appears attractive. In any event, I'll bet it involves eating lots of cabbage soup. Like most plans, I'm sure if followed faithfully, weight will be lost. You'll also probably permanently swear off ever eating cabbage soup again!

Therein lies the rub. Cabbage soup is unlikely to become the cornerstone of anyone's diet on an ongoing basis. Eventually, there will be a return to "normal," and since the diet was only a temporary measure, old habits will likely return. The result is the patient regaining their former weight. A symptom was treated but not the cause.

This conundrum reveals our first success strategy: Make no changes that you're not willing to keep for a lifetime.

Make No Changes That You're Not Willing to Keep for a Lifetime

This tactic immediately eliminates nonsensical strategies, such as the Cabbage Soup Diet. A broader example proves the point. If a person is concerned about attaining financial security, consider a strategy involving careful research of various investments and then setting aside a meaningful portion of income to commit accordingly. This regimen is followed for six weeks, after which the "investor" returns to their previous spendthrift habits. Obviously, this isn't going to work.

The problem extends further than just a soup diet. There are plenty of companies hawking meal plans for customers to follow. The company sends meals; all the customer has to do is eat what the company sends. The problem is that the customer isn't going to eat these prepackaged meals forever. The patient is effectively delegating nutritional decisions and portion sizes to a vendor. If self-governance isn't learned, the end result will be failure.

One of the dynamics that must be overcome is the notion that, having made a significant sacrifice and achieved a goal, a reward should be forthcoming. If indulging in favorite foods or taking a break from an exercise regimen experienced as miserable are still regarded as rewarding, the patient still hasn't made the leap to forming new habits designed to achieve long-term success. Indeed there should be rewards, but how about a new outfit geared to your new dimensions? Or it could be a weekend getaway, but again, be careful. Eating out is another peril.

Life is a marathon, not a sprint. Victory is often experienced by the steady tortoise versus the hare. Committing to only making permanent changes demands a more incremental approach. Let's consider an exercise regimen.

Before you take the plunge and sign up for an expensive health club membership, consider that according to Gymdesk, 18% of health club members, or about one in five, never attend. This is worse than merely not exercising and failing to attain your goals; now money is also wasted.

If considering an exercise regimen, remember, you're committing to this for the rest of your life. Can you trust yourself to go to the gym on a regular basis and sweat it out for a sustained period? Is there any indication from your past that serves as evidence that you will be able to do this?

Instead, consider just walking a little further each day. In place of orbiting the parking lot looking for the closest space, just take the first one seen. Or even make a point of taking the furthest spot. Get off the elevator a few floors early and take the stairs for the last few flights. Use the restroom furthest from your work location instead of the closest one. There is plenty of technology available to help count steps if you want to challenge yourself to increase the distance over time.

If your weight loss goals have still not been achieved, consider being more deliberate about your walking regimen. For the first time, walking could become an end in itself. In other words, you're waking nowhere. Perhaps start with a walk around the block. Keep going further if it's enjoyable and it feels like something you can commit to for the long term. Consider an accountability partner to join you.

Partnering in your success journey is an important consideration. Fundamentally, it's about knowing yourself so you can position yourself for success. For example, I prefer to work alone versus a team approach. I'm an introvert. I also seem able to commit to a routine without the need for outside help. Therefore, for me, having a workout partner would only slow my progress. But that's me. Consider the approach that makes the most sense for you.

For financial goals, partnering for success can mean something different. Often there already is a partnership—a marriage or other committed relationship. Obviously, any couple must agree on financial objectives before progress can be made. But even then, sometimes neither individual possesses the acumen to formulate and adhere to a reasonable financial plan. That might mean meeting with a financial counselor or another couple that has mastered their finances, doing online research, or exploring resources from recognized experts like Dave Ramsey. The point is to have sufficient self-awareness to know when you need help or can go it alone. The more you have failed in the past or the deeper your problems are all point to a greater need to find accountability partners. This is a good segue into our next success strategy, which is to know yourself.

Know Yourself

We've just embarked on this success journey and the first instruction is to take an incremental approach. But does this instruction always apply? Sometimes there is a call-to-action moment that is more dramatic. Sometimes, a crisis motivates an individual to abruptly make wholesale changes. Whether it's that moment when the entire weight of disastrous financial circumstances finally becomes apparent, a relationship wake-up call, or a health calamity, sometimes a person is ready to make massive, intense changes. Ultimately, only you can decide the best approach. But proceed with deliberation. Consider again Luke 14:28-30 ESV:

> For which of you, desiring to build a tower, does not first sit down and count the cost, whether he has enough to complete it? [29] Otherwise, when he has laid a foundation and is not able to finish, all who see it begin to mock him, [30] saying, 'This man began to build and was not able to finish.'

Whether an incremental approach or a radical transformation, make sure you possess the resources to follow through, be those resources financial, spiritual, psychological, or measured in terms of fortitude.

Continue in self-examination. Where do your vulnerabilities lie? I have a propensity to snack at night and I don't think I'm alone. Many graze away while watching TV or for me, while reading. Shake things up. Maybe an evening exercise routine is just the double whammy that's needed to create a new outcome and new habits.

Let's consider some success strategies that always apply.

Success Strategies

1. Stop Looking for Magic Bullets

People have been in search of a weight loss miracle cure for a long time. Recently, such miracles seem to be at hand in the form of Ozempic and other drugs. However, the long-term effects of taking these drugs are unknown. Further, our objective was to lose 20 pounds. That's different from curing chronic obesity. This book is not the remedy for a person with a serious health condition. Drugs like Ozempic aren't for people trying to lose a few pounds.

Similarly, a person waking up to realize their finances are a disaster or that retirement looms and savings are thin may be tempted by exotic returns. There is a relationship between risk and return. The temptation of high returns always comes with higher risk. The prevalence of internet financial scams is further evidence of our propensity to fall for the promise of easy money.

Sometimes, magic bullets come in a much more insidious form. Faced with a failing relationship, rather than putting in the work to revitalize a commitment made to a marriage partner before God, a person instead seeks refuge in a new relationship. For lack of self-examination, often the same problems are taken into the new coupling and serial divorce is the result.

2. Put Your Mind to Work in Your Favor

Often, when I'm working out, I may be doing 15 repetitions of an exercise. Obviously, the 15th repetition is harder than the first. It is both physiologically and psychologically difficult to make it to the 15th repetition. I can't do anything about my physiological limitations, at least not in one workout! However, I can address the psychological limitations. That's why sometimes I count backward to one, or count to three sets of five, or five sets of three or just about any other convoluted counting mechanism to get my mind off the difficulty of performing that exercise! Further, I exercise first thing in the morning because I know I'm going to be too tired at night. I even front end load the week, having the hardest workout on Monday and tapering off through the week because that's just how my mind works. I like to get the hardest tasks out of the way as early as possible, be that on a daily or weekly basis.

There are all kinds of practical applications to this strategy. For the salesperson charged with having to engage in prospecting that is distasteful, self-assess when you can be at your peak for this task and schedule accordingly. Postpone more enjoyable work as a reward for when the prospecting is done. In the area of finances, pay yourself first. Commit funds to savings or investments first before anything else. Make all other obligations subject to your saving and investing goals.

I used to include 30 minutes of cardio on a recumbent exercise bike six mornings per week. During this time, I often cleared email or tended to other business. Frequently, I would get so absorbed in these activities, I would go over the intended 30 minute limit. Then I realized there was an opportunity here. I increased the intended time from 30 minutes to 35. A five minute increase six times per week is a weekly addition of 30 minutes. I feel like I'm getting an extra cardio workout for free.

One arrangement I have with myself is that all my workouts are optional. All that's required is that I walk through the doors of the gym. Once I'm through that door, I'm under no further obligation. I can turn around and go home if I want. But since I'm already there, I may as well work out! However, I have no obligation whatsoever to complete the entire workout, achieve a new personal best, or anything else. But funny thing, once I'm there and started, I'm always able to continue with a vigorous workout.

Committing to financial goals can work the same way. A deposit can be made to a savings or investment account as soon as payroll funds become available. Alternatively, perhaps a payment is made against a debt immediately. It might be unclear just how further obligations are going to be met until the next payroll comes! However, this might be a helpful way to develop more disciplined spending habits.

Perhaps the greatest psychological win is when our new seemingly hard habits become enjoyable. Exercise can be enjoyable. Junk and convenience food can become distasteful as our palette begins to become acclimated to new habits and better food. The state of mind is vital. Consider again Philippians 4:11-13:

> Not that I am speaking of being in need, for I have learned in whatever situation I am to be content. I know how to be brought low, and I know how to abound. In any and every circumstance, I have learned the secret of facing plenty and hunger, abundance and need.

Another way to state this verse is the author, Paul, is saying that he's been rich and he's been poor, or he's been hungry and he's been full, but in all things, he has learned to be content. Learning to be content in all circumstances is one of the most difficult spiritual and psychological challenges. Let's emphasize again that this attribute is learned. If contentment is not deliberately sought and cultivated, a person is vulnerable to being a slave to forever wanting more.

We already explored the Ambition Paradox. The Ambition Paradox is about being able to simultaneously strive for more while still being content with the present. It means falling in love with the journey, not the destination. Indeed, if contentment cannot be achieved with what we have now, when something more is attained, we won't be content with that either because we have not learned to be content. Being content is learned behavior that must be deliberately developed.

Right now, I'm driving a newer vehicle. I really enjoy it. But for most of my life, I've driven some used piece of junk. A new car just didn't fit into my other financial objectives. A funny thing happened along the way. I've developed some sort of twisted enjoyment out of driving an older vehicle. I feel like I'm getting away with something every time it starts! It's nice not to have to worry about whether the vehicle is clean or not—at least on the outside. For some reason, I've got to have the interior clean enough for performing surgery. Perhaps that's my reward for driving an older car. I also can't stand to have anything less than everything in the vehicle working perfectly, even if the vehicle is older.

3. Employ the Power of Substitution

Just living a life of austerity can't be the solution or frustration will be the result. Our journey was to seek a better life, and austerity sounds like a worse one. I enjoy good food. There are certain things I'm not going to live without, like pizza, french fries, dark chocolate and dry-roasted peanuts. I may need to enjoy these things less often or in smaller quantities, but I'm not giving them up.

Consider employing the Power of Substitution. I think the Power of Substitution explains why even my older vehicles must be meticulously clean, at least on the inside. Perhaps that cleanliness substitutes for the new car experience. Ditto having everything working. Or maybe I can claim I'm a good steward of all that belongs to the Lord. It's good for the Christian to think that way, even if my own selfish interests seem to be encroaching.

I'm employing the Power of Substitution. On my own, I tend to be lazy. That's why giving my business to the Lord was one of the best decisions I ever made. By myself, it might be good enough. But if I must give an account to God for this, then it's time to stand up straight and get back to work. Or maybe all these ideas are better categorized under the mental games I'm playing with myself to keep on task. Either way, it keeps me moving.

Beware of when the Power of Substitution can be misapplied. In my opinion, opting for fat-free or sugar-free food alternatives can sometimes be a mistake. Instead of satisfying a craving, a yearning for the real thing can remain. Better to form new habits where this indulgence can be enjoyed less often in smaller quantities or both.

The Power of Substitution is strongest when good new habits are substituted for old, bad habits. We already considered one such swap, timing an exercise regimen for when we might otherwise be tempted to snack. Attacking the most burdensome or unappealing tasks first instead of indulging in procrastination is another good for bad habit swap.

Finances

The first thing to realize is that, like all other circumstances, your financial condition did not evolve overnight. Rather, spending patterns may even go back generations. You may have learned by seeing what your parents and grandparents did, for better or for worse.

The one thing that's different about finances is that sometimes, taking stock of your current condition is more involved than just looking in the mirror. If a person is seriously overweight, that can be confirmed at a glance. By contrast, there are plenty of folks with financial cancer that have no idea of their peril.

Just like a person might get a complete physical exam from a doctor before starting a diet or exercise regimen, so too the first step must be to take stock of current financial conditions. Make a list of what you own and what you owe. Create a list of committed monthly payments like rent, mortgage, utilities, subscriptions, insurance, and other minimum loan payments. Compare these monthly obligations to your after-tax income. If there is not an adequate surplus from this investigation to fund financial goals, changes will have to be made.

Getting into the details of forming a budget and a spending plan is beyond the scope of this book. Dave Ramsey is an excellent resource for those needing more specific guidance. For now, let's focus on the big picture.

It's Not About Income

I wish I could share with you how you can double or even triple your income overnight with ease. But the world is already too full of these snake oil salespeople. Consider instead the five professions most likely to make you rich. All you have to do is be a doctor, right? Dave Ramsey recently conducted a survey of 10,000 millionaires in the US to find out what they did for work and how they became affluent. The list is below. Prepare to be shocked.

1. Engineer
2. Accountant
3. Teacher
4. Manager
5. Attorney

This list underscores something I've been saying for a long time. It's not how much you make; it's how much you keep. Engineers, accountants, and teachers are among the most practical, pragmatic folks you're likely to meet. Apparently, they're frugal too. Few people go into teaching with the expectation of becoming wealthy. Yet look what happened.

Folks engaged in these occupations are rule followers. Saving and investing is just another process governed by rules that these analytical minds have no problem embracing.

The Ramsey survey went on to observe that most million-aires are first-generation—meaning they earned their wealth themselves. Inheritance is nice, but unless Bill Gates leaves you the money, learning something about how to handle finances is a must or the money may just slip through your fingers.

There's just no escaping living a controlled, disciplined existence, whether the goal be weight loss, financial security, or just about anything else. Finally, then, consider the Prosperity Paradox.

The Prosperity Paradox

The most likely way to financial security and other areas of goal attainment is to embrace frugality. Once you achieve your financial goals and can afford anything, you may find yourself not wanting anything but instead preferring a humble lifestyle. That's the Prosperity Paradox.

How to Lose 20 Pounds

We began the conversation by discussing how to lose 20 pounds. Perhaps I haven't fully delivered on that promise. Time to call in an expert. I can't think of a better expert than my son, Joel. Joel is studying to be a personal trainer. He looks like a personal trainer. He became interested in weightlifting and fitness, and in 18 months, he packed on 25 pounds of lean muscle. But he's not just disciplined about working out. He subjected his diet to a complete transformation as well.

This wasn't the incremental approach mentioned earlier. Joel went all in and has stayed all in for several years now. It's a lifestyle. But I've said too much already. I'll turn the rest of this conversation over to Joel.

Weight Loss Tips from Joel Decker

Losing weight really isn't as complicated as most people make it out to be. You simply need to calculate how many calories you consume and burn on a daily basis. The average person needs about 2,000 calories a day to maintain their weight; so if you want to lose weight, you should be eating less than that. There's 3,500 calories in a pound of fat, so if you want to lose a pound of fat every week, simply eat 1,500 calories a day and the weight will drop off consistently. It doesn't even matter if you're eating clean or not as long as you're counting your calories. There is no reason to completely abstain from your favorite indulgences so long as you adhere to your caloric limits. You will still lose the same amount of weight as someone who only eats chicken and broccoli; likewise, if you ate 2,500 calories of chicken and broccoli, you'd actually gain weight, even though you're eating healthy foods.

However, restricting yourself to just 1,500 calories a day is very hard. The 2,000 caloric maintenance required to maintain your weight I mentioned is assuming you live a sedentary lifestyle. When I lost 35 pounds in just 3 months, I was burning around 1,000 extra calories a day from lifting weights and riding my bike, which allowed me to eat more but still lose weight.

To sum it all up: watch your caloric intake. You can eat whatever you want as long as you're in a deficit (but it is easier to choose foods that are both filling and low calorie). Exercise will help as well but isn't required for weight loss.

> Every athlete exercises self-control in all things. They do it to receive a perishable wreath, but we an imperishable. So I do not run aimlessly; I do not box as one beating the air. But I discipline my body and keep it under control, lest after preaching to others I myself should be disqualified. —1 Corinthians 9:25-27 ESV

"There are no secrets to
success. It is the result of
preparation, hard work,
and learning from failure."
—Colin Powell

14

HOW TO BE SUCCESSFUL

Most books like this one will eventually get around to telling you that you have to follow your passions. I took it a bit further by calling that passion a cause. Therefore, the formula is hard work + passion = success.

Except the equation is wrong, or at least incomplete.

It goes without saying that hard work and passion are going to be instrumental for success, but there are missing ingredients. One of them is a willingness to take risks.

There are lots of people who are passionate and hard-working, but they don't have the success they want because they have not taken any chances. I related just such a person in Chapter Six, Rookie Season. I met an older gentleman at a big company who was nearing retirement. As he shared his career path and "success story" with me, all I could think was, "This is going to be me in thirty years if I don't get out of here." This gentleman was passionate and hardworking, but risk-averse.

Fear of Failure

I believe most people don't take risks because they are afraid of failure. Studies show that people will work harder to avoid pain than to experience gain. The allure of what could be by starting a business or investing in real estate just isn't enough to overcome the fear of failure should these moves go wrong.

There's a way to reverse that equation and put fear back on your side, and I've already shown you what it is. When I met that older man nearing retirement, it was like a Reality Face Punch of what my life might look like if I didn't man up and execute on my goals of getting into real estate full time and making a living being a landlord. In other words, the fear and pain of a missed opportunity was the compelling catalyst, not the appeal of a luxury lifestyle or the accumulation of material possessions.

> For God gave us a spirit not of fear but of power and love and self-control.   —2 Timothy 1:7 ESV

Respect Your Fear

I'm not going to berate anyone for being unwilling or uncomfortable taking risks. Many people have a spouse and children to consider, and the money needs to keep showing up, or lives are going to be disrupted. Sticking to a mediocre job with a bleak future can be the result. Consider 1 Timothy 5:8 ESV, But if anyone does not provide for his relatives, and especially for members of his household, he has denied the faith and is worse than an unbeliever.

Being married and having children are some of the most important responsibilities a person can have. It's not your future you're gambling with; it might be theirs. So, a healthy respect for the consequences of failing is prudent.

While I won't berate anyone for being uncomfortable taking risks, I will berate people for having loose financial practices that obliterate any possibility of starting a business or making investments. Said another way, some people's spendthrift habits are the reason they fear failure. Their financial world is already a house of cards, and any disruption to income flow precipitates immediate disaster. They lack Walking Away Money.

Walking Away Money

Have you heard about the golden rule? Forget about that do unto others stuff. The golden rule is that he who has the gold rules.

If you're employed, your boss should be a mentor, growing you and challenging you to do better. If your boss is a jerk and you're not looking for another job, it may be because you lack Walking Away Money.

Walking Away Money gives you the freedom from fear you need to take a flyer on a career change, an investment, or even starting your own business. You don't dread failure because you can afford it. If a sizeable chunk of money disappears on a failed endeavor, your kids won't starve, your mortgage won't be foreclosed, and your life will continue as before.

Keep Your Fear Working for You

The world of retail is hard at work with every kind of temptation to separate you from your cash. Here's how to fight back—amp up the consequences of every purchase. Now buying those fancy coffees means being stuck in a dead-end job forever. Getting a new outfit jeopardizes investing in your future. Getting a new car may mean postponing acquiring real estate.

Your fear is not to be avoided, it's to be cultivated. Use your fear to drive you to carefully investigate different investment or business opportunities. Take risks, but those risks should be calculated risks. Work hard to mitigate every risk you can. Don't take blind risks—that's what casinos are for.

The prudent sees danger and hides himself, but the simple go on and suffer for it. Proverbs 1:27

Mitigate Your Risk

I've been investing in real estate for nearly forty years. I'm still constructing my own income statement for any real estate I consider buying. Owing to recent explosive inflation, many of my old cost assumptions no longer apply. Instead, there is the painstaking process of getting a quote from my agent for property insurance, calling utility companies to verify costs, confirming property taxes with municipalities, and querying my waste hauling contractor for service estimates. Assumptions are made about how to market the property for rent and how much it will cost. If the property needs significant improvements—and that's nearly always the case—then contractor estimates are needed for those costs as well. A rent survey is completed to confirm income assumptions. Then we think about how to staff the operation and estimate those costs.

In short, a concerted effort is made to avoid getting blind-sided by unanticipated costs that can turn a good investment into a bad one. This effort gives us the perfect segue to the final success formula equation:

$$\text{Passion} + \text{Hard Work} + \text{Preparation} + \text{Talent} + \text{Prudent Risks} = \text{Success}$$

With talent, I've introduced another topic in the success formula that we'll get to in a minute. First, I want to show you how the pieces fit together.

Passion is what fuels the hard work necessary to engage in the preparation required to be successful. Once prepared, passion motivates us to take prudent risks. That leads us to the final ingredient, talent.

It's hard to imagine being passionate about doing something you're not good at, but an example will be illuminating. Dale Carnegie is best known for self-help books like *How to Win Friends and Influence People.* This book continues to garner sales even though it was first published in 1936. However, before publishing this and other successful nonfiction books, Carnegie tried acting and even fancied himself a novelist—vocations that never panned out. Carnegie is clearly a talented individual, but like the rest of us, not at everything.

The key, then, is to focus your efforts on those areas where your talents are greatest. However, as can be observed from the

Carnegie example, sometimes it's hard to identify where those talents lie. Once again, passion helps solve the riddle.

Take a guess about your talents and dive into a corresponding vocation like your life depends on it—in other words, with passion. If it doesn't work out, try something else. Eventually, you'll find your niche.

I love the real estate business. But along the way, I've also thrown myself into physical fitness—power lifting and body building—and music long enough and far enough to discover I don't have the innate talent to make it as an athlete or musician. I've even been to a few open mics to try my hand at stand-up comedy—talk about taking a risk! But you won't see me cracking jokes on live stream or YouTube anytime soon. While trying and failing had some awkward moments—to say the least—I can move forward in life without wondering what could have been had I never tried. You'll be the one to decide if I've got the chops to make it as a writer!

Let's do the math one last time:

Passion + Hard Work + Preparation + Talent + Prudent Risks = Success

Don't skip any steps and remember me when you hit it big.

"Have I not commanded you? Be strong and courageous. Do not be frightened, and do not be dismayed, for the Lord your God is with you wherever you go."
—Joshua 1:9 ESV

SECTION 3

A GLIMPSE OF THE FUTURE

"It's tough to make

predictions, especially

about the future."

—Yogi Berra

15

THE FUTURE OF AUTONOMOUS VEHICLES

Autonomous vehicles were all the rage once, and just around the corner. And then, just as quickly, they were gone. Seemingly.

But they are not gone at all. There are just a few more problems than anticipated. When autonomous vehicles start becoming more commonplace, the impact will be enormous. Getting it right will be important, and most of what I have heard about this future has been wrong.

Media goons think and secretly hope, that private automobiles will be a thing of the past. We will all be subscribers to ride-sharing services faster than you can say Uber. Auto sales will crater, and car companies will crash.

But this defies all logic.

While there will undoubtedly be a continued increase in ride-sharing services and in dense urban environments, car ownership may indeed decline; my prediction is that autonomous vehicles will result in more cars, not less. For it to be otherwise, it would mean that for the first time in recorded history, a product or service will become easier to use, but we will want less of it.

There will be more cars because the gold standard of transportation is still the private automobile. If cars were about nothing more than getting from A to B, then any old used econobox would do. Utility alone cannot explain the predominance of combat-ready SUVs that are about all you can buy today.

Clearly, our cars are so much more than just transportation. They are a statement about who we are, or think we are, or wish we were.

Often, meaningless statistics are cited in defense of ride-sharing services. Like the observation that our cars spend 95% or more of their time parked and not in use. My toothbrush spends 99% of its life parked in a cup next to my sink, but that doesn't mean I want to participate in a toothbrush-sharing service. Having to ride in a car previously occupied by unsupervised strangers doing who knows what is about as appealing as a public toilet or a shared toothbrush.

Autonomous cars mean that the elderly never have to give up the keys, and junior doesn't have to wait until 16 to get his or her first car. The blind and disabled can be car owners, too. That means more cars, not less.

Currently, governments worldwide are pushing for a transition to electric cars in response to climate change. Plenty of subsidies are being dished out so rich folks can buy luxury electric vehicles. Perhaps that means autonomous cars will be electric cars. Electric cars should be more affordable to fuel and maintain. It is hard to imagine now, but electric vehicles will be cheaper to buy eventually. They contain fewer parts than internal combustion vehicles and are easier to assemble.

At least, this is the theory until the Reality Face Punch encroaches on our happy place. The problem with electric cars is they require rare earth metals from China and plenty of cobalt from Africa. The mining of cobalt is rife with human rights abuses. Being beholden to the Chinese Communist Party for anything is asking for trouble. Our slavery to climate change will not accommodate these problems.

Electric cars have always had the problem of range and charge times. Those problems are going to become more complicated if we do not want to source the raw materials from thugs and communist dictators. As we shall see, the desired range of an autonomous car will be enormous. People may prefer to sleep in their car overnight for an eight-hour drive rather than taking a flight. That means a range of around 600 miles will be needed.

For decades, technological advancements in internal combustion engines have meant more horsepower from the same or smaller engine displacement. This is what consumers wanted. The consumer wanted to put the pedal to the metal and feel the sensation of raw power while pulling out in front of a semi on the freeway.

That will not be desirable for the autonomous car. Riders will be busy with laptops or applying makeup. Jackrabbit acceleration means that you jab yourself in the eye with a mascara wand. Reliability and fuel efficiency will be the order of the day. Achieving greater fuel efficiency also expands potential range. Advantage internal combustion engine.

If efficiency and reliability become the primary focus, the proliferation of engine sizes will be reduced. Manufacturers may be able to focus on a narrow range of offerings. Production costs could decline for internal combustion engines for the same reasons.

As electric vehicles gain greater acceptance, demand for gasoline will decline, leading to lower gas prices. At the same time, our existing electrical grid does not have the capacity to support a large portion of the automobile market going electric. Between the cost of added infrastructure and an increased demand, electricity prices will increase. The result will be a continued place for internal combustion engines, at least on an interim basis. Government mandates could throw these predictions off, but even the government cannot mandate an electric grid into existence that doesn't exist today. That simply takes time.

Whether electric or internal combustion, autonomous vehicles will proliferate, not evaporate.

The world will be radically transformed by autonomous vehicles. It would be impossible to predict the full impact, but we need to begin imagining a world with more cars than ever. That is why the apartments I have been developing often include two and even three-car attached garages prewired for vehicle charging. Here are a few additional potential changes autonomous vehicles may bring:

- Urban Parking Ramps may decline in value. Why pay a premium to park in an expensive parking ramp when you can dispatch your empty vehicle to cheaper parking on the outskirts? Massive stadium parking lots may gain a new revenue stream on other than game day for the same reason. But wait, will there still be the need for the stadium parking lots? Once again, the empty vehicle can just be instructed to retreat and return as needed.

- Architecture will change. Having a covered passenger drop-off point at retail and office buildings will become a must-have. Multiple drop-off points at stadiums will also be the norm. For stores and restaurants, this means less decline in business during inclement weather. Valet parking used to be exclusive territory of the wealthy. Now, the equivalent experience will be mandatory for survival of any business dependent upon their customers arriving by automobile.

- Automobiles will change. Once vehicles are autonomous, owners will engage in all manner of other activities while riding along. Anticipate cars becoming a cross between a bathroom vanity and a home office. During commute time, riders may want to do their hair and makeup or get an early start on some office work. Others will want to sleep in their cars. Why book a flight to a city six hours drive away when you can slip into comfortable clothes and snooze while your car drives itself? This will mean that flight schedules and airport traffic will change as well.

- Remote work will be impacted. Thanks to COVID, working remotely is part of the new reality. But employers are trying to summon their workers back to the office. One of the reasons remote work is valued is employee objection to commute times. Once you can work in your vehicle while it drives itself, a compromise between management and office workers has been found.

- There may be more traffic. Key to our thesis is that autonomous vehicles will mean wider use by younger, older, and even disabled users. In addition to that, roads may be clogged with empty cars! As alluded to elsewhere, your car can simply drop you off and proceed to a parking space that may be miles away, then return empty to pick you back up. It may become necessary to outlaw this practice, but this will be a programming issue. Police won't be pulling over empty cars!

- Hospitality will change. There will be new demand for a facility for a freshening up versus a night's sleep. You might be able to sleep while your car drives, but a shower in the morning would be nice. Facilities like this already exist. They are called truck stops. The parallel facility of the future is going to need to be more prolific, cleaner, more luxurious, and more accessible. Perhaps it will be combined with a dining opportunity—breakfast anyone? Imagine an entire franchised chain of facilities featuring electric car charging stations, shower facilities, dining options, laundry facilities, and a car wash.

- Retail will experience additional challenges. Brick-and-mortar stores have already been impacted by competition from online competitors. One of the biggest problems online businesses face is the last-mile delivery from the distribution centers to individual homes and offices. Imagine what it is going to be like once that last mile can be traversed by an autonomous vehicle. Delivery speed will increase while delivery costs decline.

- Government revenue streams will be disrupted. Parking tickets? Gone. Speeding tickets? Gone. This is not a small change. Estimates of annual revenue from citations run into billions of dollars.

- Insurance costs will decline. Fewer traffic accidents mean lower insurance costs. There will be fewer car thefts as well, see below.

- Personal injury litigation will decline. Fewer accidents mean fewer lawyers. It makes me cry.

- Crime will fall. Can you imagine an autonomous vehicle as your getaway driver? And your car will be a password-protected gigantic electronic gizmo—stealing it will be nearly impossible.

- Auto repair will change. An electric car can last longer. That means parts that didn't used to wear out will wear out now. Items such as seats, flooring, and consoles may require replacement. Will a vehicle take on some of the attributes of a home? Just as a home remains largely intact while it undergoes several remodels over time, will a long-lasting electric vehicle be designed to upgrade modules in the car? Or will planned obsolescence obliterate this pipe dream?

- Alcoholism will increase. This is the unintended consequence of autonomous vehicles. Sometimes, a drunk driving arrest is the Reality Face Punch someone needs to understand their drinking is out of control. With autonomous vehicles, such problems may remain hidden longer. In fact, the use of all intoxicants may increase with autonomous vehicles. Autonomous vehicles will be a boon to the adult beverage industry for the same reason.

Perhaps the greatest boon of all is productivity. According to AAA, US drivers spend 91 billion hours driving annually. In the future, all or much of that time may be captured and dedicated to doing something else.[1]

It's one of the reasons why I'm so bullish about the future. There will be unprecedented opportunities for those that are paying attention. And even for those who aren't, entrepreneurial activity will enhance everyone's life as we'll explore next in the Future of Garbage.

The heart of man plans his way, but the Lord establishes his steps.   —Proverbs 16:9 ESV

"Nothing in the world can take the place of persistence. Talent will not; nothing is more common than unsuccessful men with talent. Genius will not; unrewarded genius is almost a proverb. Education will not; the world is full of educated derelicts."

—Calvin Coolidge

16

THE FUTURE OF GARBAGE

If you're a nerd ball like me, you spend way too much time thinking about things like those great big garbage dumpsters at apartment complexes. Maybe soon, geniuses in government will mandate that diesel garbage trucks get 10% cleaner emissions in service to climate change. In the meantime, entrepreneurs are at work.

To understand how entrepreneurs are going to impact the future of garbage, we first must answer an important question: What's the largest item by volume in those garbage dumpsters? Is it food waste? Disposable diapers? Beer can pull tabs? OK, you have to be an old guy like me to even remember beer can pull tabs!

No, the largest item *by volume* in any of these containers isn't any of the above. It's air. And therein lies the opportunity.

Merely throwing stuff in the trash is old school. In the future, users will deposit trash in the solar-powered compactor/shredder attached to the dumpster. After the compactor/shredder does its thing, the refuse is distributed evenly throughout the container. As the container gets increasingly full, this internet-connected smart receptacle will begin communicating with the waste disposal contractor. The contractor will know when the receptacle is nearly full or completely full. This is vital.

Today, with conventional dumb equipment, waste disposal salespeople love to sell their landlord-customers plenty of additional capacity. The revenue stream will be measured by the size of the container and the frequency of pickup, regardless of how full or how empty the container may be.

Apartment managers are complicit in this over-capacity scheme. Capacity needs can fluctuate with time. Christmas brings greater disposal needs, as does the summer when more tenants are moving in and out. Apartment managers don't like an overflowing dumpster and the resulting mess. Therefore, they are inclined to call for a bigger container for use all year when peak capacity occurs only infrequently.

But smart containers only get emptied when they are full. Overflow is avoided. Employing the shredding and monitoring mechanisms above could reduce the frequency of pickups by up to 75%. That means that expensive capital outlays for garbage trucks are reduced by 75%. The number of trips to collect garbage is reduced by 75%. Diesel fuel consumption is cut by 75%, and the climate is better for it.[1]

But what about garbage truck driver employment? Does that go down 75%, too? More likely, it goes down 100% when the trucks are autonomously driven.

The waste-hauling contractor that is first to adopt these new technologies gains a cost advantage in the marketplace. This contractor will enjoy higher profit margins and increasing market share. But only for a while.

In time, other waste-hauling contractors will either adopt this new technology or go out of business. Then, a price war will break out. Prices for trash hauling services will fall until profit margins for trash haulers return to about what they were in the days of the old dumb containers.

That's when landlords like me experience a windfall. Waste hauling costs go down, and rents remain the same. I wish you could see me snickering and rubbing my hands together like Charles Montgomery Burns from *The Simpsons*. Excellent!

But alas, this windfall is also fleeting. Because the rental market is also competitive, over time, rents either decline or increase more slowly. Margins for landlords return to where they were before the smart containers were adopted.

Who, then, is the final beneficiary? The tenant living in those apartments. Never mind about the waste hauling company that pioneered this new technology at considerable risk. Never mind the landlord who had the vision to be an early adopter of this new technology. The final beneficiary is always the end consumer, who often has nothing to do with any of it.

This is why our standard of living continues to increase almost as if by magic. For the final consumer, it is unseen. It is without risk and without effort.

For the lucky entrepreneur who solves these kinds of problems, an economic windfall awaits, even if it is temporary. This windfall is concentrated in those few lucky creators wise enough to bring exciting new ideas to market. These inventors and their newfound wealth are often quite visible.

Nearly invisible is the increment in wealth gain that happens to every consumer enjoying the new technology. But cumulatively, the wealth gain experienced by all consumers benefiting from the new technology far surpasses the wealth concentrated in the inventors. Never mind that politicians will seek to divide us by insinuating that the concentration of wealth in these creative contributors is somehow unfair. Politicians will want to punish these contributors with high taxes and onerous regulations.

Often, there are unintended additional benefits. A few years ago, cities were concerned about the accumulation of waste. There didn't seem to be a remedy, and the problem was only getting worse. The waste accumulating? Horse manure. The problem was solved by Henry Ford and the automobile.

The problems that vex us today are unlikely to be solved by politicians or bureaucrats. They are more likely to be solved by tinkerers and dreamers in pursuit of an opportunity. And you and I will be the better for it.

One More Step Toward a Brighter Garbage Future

One final thought before we leave this illustrious topic. We should never allow the same business that owns the landfills to own the garbage trucks. This kind of vertical integration is the current status quo. If you own the landfill, you can increase the tipping charge to any other garbage collection contractor until that contractor is pushed out of business. Then, this contractor is forced to sell out to the vertically integrated waste hauler. As the vertically integrated waste hauler eliminates the competition, prices rise, and service quality deteriorates.

This is not theoretical. One of the vertically integrated waste hauling contractors where I live has high prices, ridiculous fines, and terrible service. It is so bad that this company has been in the news. Municipalities relying on this integrated waste hauler for single-family waste removal have fined the company or turned to other vendors.

To avoid these bullies, landfills should be regulated like a public utility. Tipping fees should be the same for any garbage hauler seeking to use the landfill. The landfill operator cannot also be in the waste-hauling business. The result will be a plethora of small business garbage truck operators seeking to win business from beleaguered landlords like me, sick of their treatment at the hands of these monopolistic thugs. And happiness shall be known throughout the land.

Before we go too far savaging these integrated waste haulers, we should remember the Goodwill Paradox. The people working there are goodwill people. I know some of them. Perhaps leadership at this company is to be commended. They have been able to achieve a monopoly and corresponding monopoly profits. I have seen reports in the financial press holding out this company as a Wall Street darling.

But whatever success leadership at this company has achieved, it has come at the expense of their employees and customers. Customers are mad, and employees are getting an ear full. In the end, monopoly power is not good for anyone.

My advice for reconfiguring the waste hauling industry may be little more than trash. But thanks to the creative genius of entrepreneurs, the future looks bright even if you're a couch potato.

"Behold, I am doing a new thing; now it springs forth, do you not perceive it? I will make a way in the wilderness and rivers in the desert."   —Isaiah 43:19 ESV

"
"Success is not final, failure is

not fatal: it is the courage

to continue that counts."

—Winston Churchill
"

17

A REALITY FACE PUNCH RESCUE PLAN FOR YOUNG PEOPLE

There has never been a generation of young people that have been sold out like Gen Z. They face sky-high college tuition costs, but that's not all. Home prices have exploded, and now interest rates are at 40-year highs. If the American dream was to get an education as a springboard to home ownership, this dream would become a nightmare if not a Reality Face Punch.

The consequences will be far-ranging. Saddled with unprecedented school debt and unable to acquire a home, young people are putting off having children until later and later—even never. The US is fortunate to have robust immigration to compensate for the lower birth rates in the native population. Otherwise, the US would join the many other nations suffering from declining populations and decades-long economic malaise, like Japan.

Being a parent has been one of the greatest joys of my life. That, as a nation, we have acted to put this experience out of reach for so many is unconscionable.

Solving the Housing Crisis

There are solutions to high home prices, such as standard-izing building codes and streamlining the approval process to reduce the time, cost, and risk associated with getting housing units approved by various government agencies.

But for real progress in slashing home prices, the government should sponsor a genius grant. Budget for a substantial cash prize for any person or group that can demonstrate a replicable housing format at no more than $100 per square foot. A 2,000-square-foot home would cost only $200,000 to build. These homes should resemble traditional housing, be durable, and low maintenance.

When President Kennedy challenged the nation to go to the moon, he famously said, "We choose to go to the Moon in this decade and do the other things, not because they are easy, but because they are hard." The US pioneered the way to the moon on July 20, 1969. Stepping out onto the surface for the first time, Neil Armstrong said, "That's one small step for man, one giant leap for mankind." It was achieved with 1960s technology when cars were death traps running on leaded gas.

When the military needs a new weapon, they circulate an RFP—a request for proposal. The military specifies what they want this new hardware to be able to do, and private industry may respond accordingly. The result is a military that is the envy of the world.

Similarly, the US Government should offer a substantial prize to anyone who can demonstrate a home that can be produced in any quantity at $100 per square foot, as discussed earlier. Properly incentivized, private industry could respond to the challenge. If successful, the economic boom that would flow from such a breakthrough would be historic.

A deeper dive into solving the high cost of housing is beyond the scope of this chapter. Let's turn our focus to the high cost of a college education.

Solving the Education Cost Crisis

There are two broad solution sets to address this problem. The first set of solutions involves wide sweeping policy changes that we can't count on or control. However, the second set of solutions directly addresses key strategies for navigating the tuition crisis.

Understanding the Problem

Why is an education so expensive? One reason is the prolif-eration of borrowing. In the 1970s, few borrowed to obtain an education. Government wanted to place colleges within reach of more students and expanded eligibility for Pell Grants and other sources of funding.[1]

One can reasonably conclude that the policy was effective. Students that would have previously been priced out of a college were now able to attend. Or in other words, there was a debt fueled increase in demand that outstripped the supply of class-room space, enabling schools to increase prices.

Another reason is purely the willingness to pay for the experience. Universities now include water parks, rock climbing walls, elaborate cafeteria menus, massive gyms and recreation centers, beach clubs, lazy rivers, ski resorts, and stunning architecture and landscapes. They have this because the schools are trying to compete for customers, and the customers are willing to pay.

Then there is administrative bloat. The California Institute of Technology, Duke University, and the University of California, San Diego, all have more non-faculty personnel on campus than students.[2] While these schools are particularly egregious, administrative growth has exploded across all mainstream institutions.

Administrative bloat is exasperated by salary bloat at the executive level. Stephen Klasko at Thomas Jefferson University made $8.4 million in total compensation in 2020. Charles Monahan must be jealous, he only got $4.5 million from the skinflints at MCPHS University. Has anyone even heard of MCPHS? Shirley Jackson had to limp by on $4.2 million at Rensselaer Polytechnic Institute. Lee Bollinger was the 10th highest paid at Columbia University, clocking in at $2.4 million.[3]

Others blame states for cutting back on support of public universities. During the Great Recession, some states faced budget gaps and decreased spending for higher education.

Then, there is degree proliferation from the college industrial complex. Fresh from the I'm not making this up department, what did we do before university training was available in:

1. Auctioneering. It's kind of like engineering without all the pesky math.
2. Bagpipe Studies. It's a real gas.
3. Costume Technology. My experience every morning when I get dressed.
4. Entertainment Design. What I look like after I'm dressed.
5. Fermentation Sciences. Because we need another excuse for drinking beer.
6. Floral Management. Graduates are eligible to pursue a master's in basket weaving.
7. Golf Course Management. Let's see, mow the lawn, rake the sand trap, now what?
8. Leisure Studies. A crash course in contradiction management is a prerequisite.
9. Metalsmithing. Because shop is no longer offered in high school and you flunked out of buggy whip making.
10. Puppet Arts. Hopefully, there's no strings attached.
11. Turfgrass Sciences. For when reading the back of a bag of fertilizer just isn't enough.
12. Wilderness and Adventure Studies. It's easy to get lost in the woods in this one.
13. Wildlife Studies. This either has something to do with animals, or else it's what's happening on campus on the weekends.
14. Astrobiology. The study of life on other planets so we can better understand the folks who dreamed up all these majors.

Policy Solutions

Policy solutions become easy once the problem is well understood. Remedies include expanded classrooms, better transparency, and changes to student loan underwriting.

More Classrooms

College tuition is a classic debt-fueled bubble. As I write this, some politicians want to forgive student debt. Never mind that the only entity that can ever forgive a debt is the institution that made the loan in the first place. What the government really wants is to stick taxpayers with the bill. This makes chumps out of the people who paid their own way or elected to skip school over concerns about the cost. And it's also more of the same—easy money thrown at colleges and universities. The result will be even higher tuition costs and more loan forgiveness in the future.

Instead, flood the market with classrooms. Classroom capacity can be expanded by about 50% without building anything new. Typically, universities are only in session for eight months per year. Why not operate year-round? That's not to say students would have to attend all year. Students can attend at their convenience, even if they prefer to follow a traditional schedule. The more industrious may prefer to participate all year and graduate sooner. Perhaps the summer semesters will be cheaper to entice students.

More Teachers

Tenure was intended to protect instructors so professors could speak their minds without fear of repercussion to preserve the diversity of thought on campuses. These good intentions have failed. According to Boston Magazine, in New England, liberal professors outnumber conservatives 28 to one.[4]

Instead of teaching how to think, schools are indoctrinating students in what to think. Therefore, end tenure. It should be no more difficult to terminate a professor from a university than it is to dismiss any white-collar employee in private industry. However, what is needed is not merely a diversity of thought but a plethora of teachers.

While classrooms can be expanded up to 50% just by utilizing existing infrastructure all year, more teachers will be needed to staff this additional capacity. To attract more and better teachers, change teaching prerequisites. There are plenty of superb instructors in private industry that lack a teaching credential that nonetheless have mastery in a particular subject and a gift for conveying ideas to others. There should be the opportunity for elites in industry, business, medicine, science, and other fields to have a sort of second career in retirement teaching at a university.

Transparency

The FDA requires that packaged food include a list of ingredients and a breakdown of calories, carbohydrates, fats, and protein among other details. An education costing tens of thousands of dollars must be equally transparent.

Schools should be required to report what percent of any freshman class graduates within four, five and six years. The report should also include the cost of that education and the percentage of graduates that have a job within their major in six and 12 months after graduation. The report should include the wages those graduates are earning as well.

Today, credit card statements include a projection of how long it will take to pay off the balance if only the minimum payment is made and the total of all those payments over time. Our colleges need to be equally transparent.

In short, there should be no mystery about the complete cost of an education, the probability of graduating and the benefits of completing the degree in terms of job placement and wages.

Debt Underwriting

Colleges and universities should be the ones underwriting student loans and lending their own money or at least guaranteeing the loans. Now schools will have some skin in the game. Should a student get a $100,000 loan to complete their degree in Leisure Studies? Will they ever be able to pay that back? Let the universities decide and lend their own money accordingly. Car companies often have a lending division to help their customers finance their vehicles, so why can't schools do the same?

Do away with the bankruptcy prohibitions for student debt. Today, too many students have the worst of all possible worlds.

They have crushing debt but no degree. Much of the cost of an education has been incurred but not the benefits. The prohibitions on bankruptcy turn these young people into indentured servants to the college industrial complex.

Student loan forgiveness is a one size fits all remedy. Even students with excellent jobs earning high wages in their field of study may see their loans forgiven. These students would ordinarily have no trouble paying back their loans. The former students most in need of relief are those who incurred substantial debt but never graduated. These forgiveness proposals are more about buying votes than extending relief where it's needed. Further, there is already a remedy available to borrowers who find their debts insurmountable—bankruptcy.

No doubt, making schools responsible for making student loans and lifting bankruptcy prohibitions will result in fewer student loans being made. Those cheaper summer sessions are looking more attractive all the time.

While policy changes like the above are interesting, they aren't within our control. What's needed is a set of strategies that can be implemented right now—An Apollo Solution. Let's investigate.

An Apollo Solution for Education

1. Don't Go

When I graduated from high school in 1981, there was a simple success formula. Get a degree. Any degree. With a degree, you gained access to the professional job market, which meant better working conditions and higher pay and benefits. Without a college education, job prospects were poor.

A great deal has changed in the last forty-plus years. Everyone knows the cost of college has increased dramatically. What's not talked about as much is the decline in the quality of that education. According to a recent Wall Street Journal article, students spend about 50% less time studying or in class, but they are three times more likely to earn an A than their peers in 1961. And a grade of A is the most common grade in schools countrywide.[5]

We already discussed whether universities are more likely to teach what to think than how to think. Many students feel pressure to keep quiet about their opinions lest they fall victim to the group think mob.[6] And worse, antisemitism is rampant through many institutions of supposed higher learning.

Further, even in a hot job market in 2023, half of college graduates found themselves in jobs that don't require a degree.[7] Yet, those student loans still have to be repaid.

In the meantime, plenty of high paying jobs in the trades are going unfilled, stifling construction of new homes and other areas of commerce. 90% of construction companies in the US have difficulty finding qualified workers according to the Associated General Contractors of America. The Georgetown Center on Education and the Workforce reports there are 30 million jobs nationally paying an average of $55,000 per year that don't require a bachelor's degree.[8] Many of these jobs have an apprenticeship or journeyman track that allow workers to earn while they learn.

2. Have Clear Goals

Years ago, perhaps it made sense to go to college to "find yourself," even if you had no idea what you wanted to do. Such an indulgence is an unaffordable poor strategy for most people today. Having clear goals for an education is a good start on living a directed, purposeful life. Having clear goals is not something that ends at graduation. If you know you want to be a physician, teacher, CPA, engineer, or lawyer, those vocations require appropriate credentials and an education is warranted. Be cautious about more spurious degrees.

3. Insist on Transparency

A starting point for goal setting is graduation itself. We may never see the policies of transparency outlined earlier, but you can insist upon them as you research which institution to attend. Investigate and ask questions. You should know what percentage of an incoming freshman class graduates in four, five and six years. Find out what the total cost of the education is likely to be including adjustments for still rising tuition rates. Don't allow yourself to be blown away by elite facilities, beautiful landscaping and amenities like rock walls and fitness centers. Stop at or call the placement office and ask some direct questions about employment rates, and whether recent graduates got jobs in their field and what those jobs paid. Insist on detailed, clear answers or move on.

4. Approach Debt with Caution

The Bible says in Proverbs 22:7 ESV The rich rules over the poor, and the borrower is the slave of the lender. This truth is particularly true with student loans that are exempt from bankruptcy relief. Bankruptcy helps level the playfield between borrower and lender. A lender is more likely to renegotiate loan terms for a struggling borrower when they know the debtor can declare bankruptcy. But without such protection, the lender is holding all the cards.

This means that financing your education is another offshoot of those clear goals. There must be a sober calculus of the total debt required, what the payments will be like and how long those payments will have to be made before the debt is retired.

Make sure you explore every grant, scholarship, subsidy, or work-study program available. The financial aid office should be able to help. Consider beyond your immediate family for loans or outright gifts toward an education.

5. Know You Can Complete Your Degree Before You Begin

The worst possible outcome is to be saddled with school debt without graduating. Much of the cost has been incurred, but none of the benefits. Approximately 40% of students that take out loans do not graduate. These borrowers are more likely to default on their loans, have lower lifetime earnings, and face higher rates of unemployment.[9]

Consider what the Bible says in Luke 14:28-30 ESV: For which of you, desiring to build a tower, does not first sit down and count the cost, whether he has enough to complete it? [29] Otherwise, when he has laid a foundation and is not able to finish, all who see it begin to mock him, [30] saying, 'This man began to build and was not able to finish.

6. College Isn't the Only Way to Get an Education

A college education can be a transformative experience that opens the door to extraordinary opportunities. You may make lifelong friends. But it's not for everyone and the cost is not worth it for some or even many. Whether or not you pursue formal education, one dynamic is far more important—a thirst for knowledge.

The world is simply too fast-paced and competitive to ever stop learning. The victory will go to the intellectually curious. Whether you get a degree or not, lifelong learning is a must and there have never been better opportunities to pursue education. Intensive bootcamps quickly prepare learners for opportunities in coding, digital marketing, graphic design, and project management. Look for the topics covered in boot camps to expand with the need for specialty expertise. Massive Open Online Courses (MOOC) can feature the best, most entertaining educators addressing various topics. Likewise, topics covered in MOOCs will expand with time. Even You Tube is available for on the job solutions.

Today's results driven world is ready for new ideas and problem solvers. Academic credentials may remain important to legacy institutions and large corporations, but for bootstrap entrepreneurs, effectiveness in the moment is your PhD.

For I know the plans I have for you, declares the Lord, plans for welfare and not for evil, to give you a future and a hope.   —Jeremiah 29:11 ESV

SECTION 4

FLYING HIGH, STAYING GROUNDED

"For what does it profit a

man to gain the whole world

and forfeit his soul?"

—Mark 8:36 ESV

18

IN THE RED ZONE

Jack Welch was the CEO of the General Electric Company for twenty years, from 1981 to 2001. During his leadership, the company's value increased 4000%. That's not a typo; that's four thousand percent. The split-adjusted stock price went from $.51 per share to $24.32. $10,000 invested in GE shares at the beginning of Welch's tenure would have turned into more than $915,000 by the time he retired. Fortune Magazine named Welch "Manager of the Century" in 1999.

During the Welch era, GE was a massive conglomerate of unrelated businesses. One of Welch's success principles was that every GE division had to be number one or number two in their industry or face sale or closure. As a result, over 200 factories were shuttered and employees released, earning Welch the nickname "Neutron Jack." GE employment numbered 411,000 before Welch took over as CEO. Four years later, the ranks had been thinned to 299,000.

Upon retirement, Jack Welch did what many good CEOs do—he wrote a book, *Jack: Straight from the Gut*. This book did so well that Jack Welch did what many best-selling authors do—he wrote another book, this one called *Winning*.

In *Winning*, Welch explained the reason for writing the book. As he made public appearances and gave speeches, he realized from the questions he was asked that what people wanted to know more than anything else was how to win, hence the name of the book. He logically organized the inquiries he received into various chapters in the book.

There was one final chapter where Welch lumped together all the questions that defied organization. In this chapter, an audience member listening to a Welch presentation inquired whether Welch felt he would go to heaven. Jack Welch nimbly sidestepped the question by saying, "Well, I sure hope that's long-range planning!"

I admire Mr. Welch for being so quick on his feet! But I wonder what the honest answer would be. On the one hand, Jack Welch did a world of good. He remade GE into one of the world's largest corporations. In doing so, he made millions for stock market investors and GE employees smart enough to participate in the company stock ownership program.

But what about his personal life? Jack Welch was divorced twice and married three times. As CEO, Welch developed a personnel policy of annually eliminating the bottom-performing ten percent of all employees, regardless of absolute performance. Those first two wives must have been underperforming!

More recently, GE has fallen on hard times. GE was a charter member of the Dow Jones Industrial Average in 1896 and a member continuously from 1907 to 2018. However, by 2018, the ruin and calamity at GE led to the company being removed from the DJIA. This misfortune occurred under the leadership of CEO Jeff Immelt, the direct successor to Jack

Welch. With the more recent difficulties for GE, Jack Welch's tenure has been called into question.

So, how do the scales of justice balance for Jack Welch? Mr. Welch passed away on March 1, 2020. Did he make it to heaven? Did the good outweigh the bad? Or is there some other standard? While it's entertaining to consider Mr. Welch's final destiny, there's a question that is far more interesting. Where will you go when you die?

Where Will You Go When You Die?

You can be the CEO of a vast corporation or a humble employee working in a tiny cubicle. Maybe you're just someone reading this book. Regardless, one day, you are going to have to answer that question.

I wrote this book to help you achieve your goals. What are your objectives? The Bible has a caution for us:

> For what does it profit a man to gain the whole world and forfeit his soul?   —Mark 8:36 ESV

Whatever you might pine for, it's included in gaining the whole world. Is it your dream to win a gold medal and ascend the peaks of athletic excellence? That's included in gaining the whole world. Maybe you just want to get out of debt or achieve financial independence. Or maybe you would like to make Elon Musk look like a piker standing next to your mountain of money. Whatever degree of financial net worth you may be seeking, that's in there too.

Maybe you want to fill the stadiums so people can see you do your thing. That's included. There is no dream, no aspiration, no ambition or desire that is not entirely encapsulated in gaining the whole world.

As I write this, Jack Welch has been dead for over four years. Twenty years from now, fifty years from now, pick a number of years from now, Jack Welch will still be dead. Eternity is a long time, and Hell is the wrong place to spend it. Should you achieve whatever dreams you aspire to but die and wind up in Hell, there is no way for me to sugarcoat this for you. You are a loser. Talk about a Reality Face Punch!

A Spiritual Survey

How is it for you? Does the good outweigh the bad? I have been asking questions like this for 25 years. I have gone from door to door, speaking to strangers. I have been to thousands of homes. I have talked to hundreds if not thousands of people.

Talking to all those people was like taking a survey. Most people I spoke to weren't certain of going to heaven. But the Bible says this:

These things have I written … that ye may know that ye have eternal life…   —1 John5:13 KJV

The reason I wrote this book is to share how people can be 100% certain of their eternal destination. Consider one of my favorite passages from the Bible in Ephesians 2:8-9 KJV:

For by grace are ye saved through faith; and that not of yourselves: it is the gift of God: Not of works, lest any man should boast.

I've been misleading you, asking whether the good outweighs the bad when heaven is a free gift. There's a lot of information in Ephesians 2:8-9, so let's dig into some of the details. The verse starts out talking about "for by grace...." Grace means a gift you haven't earned and don't deserve. Here's the gift that God was talking about:

... the gift of God is eternal life ...

—Romans 6:23 KJV

So far, so good! But the verse goes on: For by grace are ye saved ....

What does it mean to be saved? If a person is going to be saved, they must be saved from something. In this case, they're being saved from having to go to Hell! Now, why do we have to talk about that? The truth is Jesus talked more about Hell than he did about Heaven. We know in Heaven, no sin gets in. We know that because in Genesis 18:25 KJV, the Bible says, "Shall not the Judge of all the earth do right?"

God Is the Judge

God is the Judge of all the world. He made the world, He gets to be the Judge. And God is holy and perfect and cannot have sin in His presence.

"You are of purer eyes than to behold evil, And cannot look on wickedness."   —Habakkuk 1:13a NKJV

Therefore, you shall be perfect, as your heavenly Father is perfect.   —Matthew 5:48 NASB

God has set an impossible standard of perfection for us. When we die, God will not compare us to other people. He will compare us to Himself and find you and me lacking. The Bible says in Romans 3:23 KJV, "For all have sinned and come short of the glory of God." God's glory is a manifestation of his perfection.

All this talk about sin, death, and Hell is sobering. But this verse in Ephesians has wonderful news, let's see what it says:

For by grace are ye saved through faith...
                —Ephesians 2:8-9 KJV

Faith is the solution—faith is the answer! But we just can't have faith, faith demands an object. To have faith means to believe, trust or depend. So in this case, we believe in, trust in, depend on, have faith in that when Jesus went to the cross, He didn't just die for the sins of the world, He died for your sins and mine. It was individual and personal. Your sins and mine put Jesus on that cross and made the cross necessary.

...without the shedding of blood there is no forgiveness of sins.   —Hebrews 9:22 ESV

That Jesus would lay down His life for sinners like me and you is incredible. But He didn't stop there. Three days later, He rose again, proving He was God, conquering sin, death, and

Hell. It is the greatest story in history. And it is a story motivated by God's love for us:

> For God so loved the world, that he gave his only begotten Son, that whosoever believeth in him should not perish, but have everlasting life.   —John 3:16 KJV

> But God commendeth (demonstrated) his love toward us, in that, while we were yet sinners, Christ died for us.
> —Romans 5:8 KJV

Think about this for a moment. If there were some other way we could get into heaven—say by belonging to a particular church, engaging in various religious rituals, adhering to a stringent moral code, or doing good deeds or works—then God is either stupid or cruel or both. Because why would God let His Son die on the cross if there were some other way we could get to Heaven?

But there is no other way. Jesus Himself said in John 14:6 ESV, "I am the way, and the truth, and the life. No one comes to the Father except through me." Jesus isn't one of the ways or *a* way, He is *the* way, there is only one way. Jesus is the way.

When Jesus was hanging on the cross, He had a few final words to share with us, and they are recorded in John 19:30: "It is finished." I'm so glad Jesus said, "It is finished," and not, "The rest is up to you!"

If you live in the US, you probably know something about Jesus. That He died on a cross is likely not new information. But we are not having a history lesson. Consider what the Bible says in James 2:19 KJV. Thou believest that there is one God; thou doest well: the devils also believe and tremble.

Satan and his minions know all about Jesus. They would even agree He died on the cross, but they are not going to Heaven! It is not what you know in your head, it's what you believe in your heart. It's what you're depending on, what you're trusting in, what you have faith in—that Jesus died for our sins that we could gain eternity.

Let's consider again the verse in Ephesians 2:8-9 KJV in its entirety:

> For by grace are ye saved through faith; and that not of yourselves: it is the gift of God: Not of works, lest any man should boast.

I love that last part! When we get to Heaven, there will be no boasting. We will know it was everything that He did and nothing that we did.

Are You Ready to Be Saved?

Are you ready to be saved? What must anyone do to be saved from having to go to Hell and instead gain entrance to Heaven? Simply this: understand and believe that when Jesus went to the cross, he took the punishment for our sins that you and I deserved. The Bible says that the wages of sin is death. Jesus took on that death on our behalf. He was the substitutional, sacrificial lamb.

If you are ready to be saved, there is nothing you must do. You don't have to go to church, you don't have to walk an aisle. Any of those things would be a work. All you must do is have a simple, childlike faith in what Jesus did on the cross, knowing that it was your sin that he died for, too. And that death on the cross was the complete payment for all your sins. That death was where the payment was made for the free gift of eternal life. Here are some supporting verses:

> ... Sirs, what must I do to be saved? 31. And they said, "Believe in the Lord Jesus Christ, and you will be saved..."   —Act 16: 30-31

> Not by works of righteousness which we have done, but according to his mercy he saved us ...   —Titus 3:5

While eternal life may be free for you and me, there was a high price paid for it. Indeed the highest price that ever could or will be paid for anything. Consider 1 Corinthians 7:23: You were bought with a price....

This verse makes no attempt to describe the price that was paid because there are no words in human language adequate to describe this price. There was never a higher price paid for anything, there are not enough zeros to measure the amount. Having paid such a price and having made this free gift available to all, is there any wonder that God is angry with sinners that have rejected Him and the free gift he has made available to all?

Are You Ready to Trust In Jesus for Your Eternity?

Are you ready to be saved? The Bible says this: Whosoever shall call upon the name of the Lord shall be saved. Romans 10:13. KJV

Please consider how radical this verse would have been when first heard. Consider just the first word, whosoever. Throughout history, people have nearly always been tribal. If you came from another place, had different cultural traditions, looked different or had different color skin, you may not be accepted, or far worse.

We are just coming to the realization that all people are created equal. We still struggle to implement the idea. By contrast, God has always been an equal opportunity God before anyone ever thought of the concept. "Whosoever shall call upon the name of the Lord shall be saved" is the boldest diversity and inclusion statement ever made! God does not care where you came from, what you look like, or even what you have done. He wants to forgive you and welcome you as one of His own.

The Sinner's Prayer

Many Christians believe you have to say the sinner's prayer to be saved. The sinner's prayer goes something like this:

Dear God, I know I am a sinner. The best way I know how I ask you to forgive me of all my sins and give me the free gift of eternal life. I am ready to trust in Jesus alone for my eternity. Jesus, thank you for saving me. Amen.

There is nothing wrong with praying a prayer like this one. Jesus certainly encouraged prayer. Jesus was not afraid to tell us how to pray and to pray specifically. When the disciples asked Jesus how to pray, Jesus gave them a specific prayer they could pray that we know today as the Lord's prayer. It begins this way, "our Father, who art in Heaven, hallowed be thy name, thy kingdom come, thy will be done, on earth as it is in Heaven ...."

Many people recognize this prayer. Jesus certainly wants people to be saved. So why didn't Jesus give us a specific sinner's prayer to pray? He never gave us such a prayer, but Jesus did tell us to believe.

Whoever believes in the Son has eternal life ...
—John 3:36 ESV

For this is the will of my Father, that everyone who looks on the Son and believes in him should have eternal life, and I will raise him up on the last day.
—John 6:40 ESV

And they said, "Believe in the Lord Jesus, and you will be saved ...." —Acts 16:31

Therefore, we must believe. If we had to pray, even that would be a work. You can pray the sinner's prayer if you like. But you will be saved because you believe. We are not trusting in a prayer, we are trusting in Jesus!

Your Life After Salvation

At the cross, your sins were forgiven. It's important to understand that while you were forgiven for your sins, you weren't cured of the propensity to sin. You are still a sinner. Even saved people that are on their way to Heaven still sin. This is an important concept that we need to address.

Many Christians believe that you must repent of your sins. Indeed, the Bible says this:

> …except ye repent, ye shall all likewise perish.
> —Luke 13:3 and Luke 13:5

The verse seems to be saying that unless you quit sinning, you will perish, or go to Hell.

But can anyone really quit sinning? What about the wicked thoughts and the idle words? What about the addict who cannot control his substance abuse?

The problem is our understanding of the word repent. In the modern vernacular, we associate the word with the need to quit doing wrong or to be sorry about our transgressions. But in the Bible, it more accurately means to change one's mind. We know this to be true because the Bible even refers to God repenting! Consider this verse in Jonah 3:10 KJV:

> And God saw their works, that they turned from their evil way; and God *repented* (emphasis added) of the evil, that he had said that he would do unto them; and he did it not.

Think about this. If we use the common definition of repenting, then a holy and perfect God is alluding to having made mistakes He regrets. But in the Bible, to repent usually means to change one's mind. Now, the previous passage in Jonah makes sense.

Let's look at the full context of the story to gain a complete understanding. God sent Jonah to a place called Nineveh because the people there were wicked. God planned to wipe them off the face of the earth unless they listened to Jonah and changed their ways. In fact, Jonah preached, the people changed and God repented, or changed his mind, about his plans to wipe out Nineveh.

There are plenty of examples in the Bible of God repenting. Here's another in Exodus 32:14 KJV:

And the Lord repented of the evil which he thought to do unto his people.

In this passage, God intended to punish the Israelites for their disobedience, but after Moses pleaded with God, God changed His mind about administering the discipline previously considered.

Indeed, God wants us to repent too. In fact, repentance is required. But it is the repentance that reflects a change of mind, not the cessation of wrongdoing. In other words, God wants us to quit trusting in our religion, our church membership, the money we gave and the good things that we did and instead change our minds to trust and depend only on Jesus' finished work on the cross. It's not a little bit of Jesus and a little bit of me. It's by faith alone in Christ alone that gains access to heaven.

Getting Saved Isn't Fire Insurance!

However, neither is being saved like getting fire insurance. Romans 6:1-2 KJV tells us so:

What shall we say then? Shall we continue in sin, that grace may abound?[2] God forbid. How shall we, that are dead to sin, live any longer therein?

Finally, we have the full understanding of repentance. It means to change our minds to stop trusting in good works or religion to be saved and instead trust in what Jesus did on the cross. While we have changed our minds about where we place our trust, we also agree with God that our sin is abhorrent and wish to desist from it and obey God.

Can a Person Lose Their Salvation?

There is more good news. Some Christians believe you can lose your salvation. But how could this be? How can one have eternal life only for a little while? Consider these verses that underscore the gift of eternal life God has extended to all, some of which we have reviewed before:

"For God so loved the world, that he gave his only Son, that whoever believes in him should not perish but have eternal life.   —John 3:16 ESV

For the wages of sin is death, but the free gift of God is eternal life in Christ Jesus our Lord.
                              —Romans 6:23 ESV

Truly, truly, I say to you, whoever hears my word and believes him who sent me has eternal life. He does not come into judgment, but has passed from death to life.
                              —John 5:24 ESV

Whoever believes in the Son has eternal life; whoever does not obey the Son shall not see life, but the wrath of God remains on him.   —John 3:36 ESV

When you are saved, the transformation is permanent. Once saved, there is no sin you could ever commit that would consign you to Hell. The Bible makes this clear:

And I give unto them eternal life; and they shall never perish, neither shall any man pluck them out of my hand.   —John 10:28 KJV

This was Jesus speaking. He is saying that no person can take away the ones who have eternal life. No person includes you. There is nothing you can do to spoil your salvation. There is nothing you or anyone can do to separate you from the love of God. Consider Romans 8:38-39 ESV:

For I am sure that neither death nor life, nor angels nor rulers, nor things present nor things to come, nor powers, [39] nor height nor depth, nor anything else in all creation, will be able to separate us from the love of God in Christ Jesus our Lord.

Once saved, you are always saved, just as once you are born, you are forever the child of your parents. Perhaps you will one day have a falling out with your parents and never speak to or see them again. Yet you will still be their child. Nothing can change that. Similarly, once a child of God, always a child of God. Many people believe that we are all God's children. This is not correct. We are all God's creation, but there is a prerequisite to becoming a child of God. That prerequisite is belief in Jesus.

But as many as received him [Jesus], to them gave he power to become the sons of God, even to them that believe on his [Jesus] name.   —John 1:12 KJV

Repent and Be Saved

We began our exploration with a spiritual survey—an inquiry into what you were trusting in to get to Heaven. Have you repented and accepted the free gift of eternal life, which is to say, changed your mind from what you were trusting in before and agreed with God about your sin? I hope that, having read this, you are trusting in Jesus alone for your eternal life. If that is a step you have taken because of reading this chapter, I would encourage you to contact me at saved@davidjdecker. com. It would be an inspiration to me and I promise I will pray for you.

Being saved is the beginning of the Christian life. There is so much more to the journey. There are mysteries to be revealed in the next chapter.

"What no eye has seen, nor ear heard, nor the heart of man imagined, what God has prepared for those who love him"   —1 Corinthians 2:9 ESV

"

"Now we have received not

the spirit of the world, but the

Spirit who is from God, that

we might understand the

things freely given

us by God."

—1 Corinthians 2:12 ESV

"

19

REVEALING A MYSTERY

Revealing a Mystery

If you have just made a decision to trust Christ with your eternity for the first time, many would say you are a new Christian. There is something unique that happens the moment a person is saved. The Holy Spirit of God takes up residence in their soul.

Since I have been present when many people made the decision to trust Christ, I can tell you that sometimes there is a visible reaction to the person receiving the Holy Spirit. Some people feel joy or euphoria. Others experience a sense of peace. Some feel relieved. But in my experience, most people feel nothing at all. How do we know then that something has changed, that the Holy Spirit is now present? Put Him to the test! The Holy Spirit of God is referred to as the comforter:

> But the Comforter, which is the Holy Ghost, whom the Father will send in my name, he shall teach you all things, and bring all things to your remembrance, whatsoever I have said unto you.   —John 14:26 KJV

I heard a pastor challenge a class, saying, "Isn't it something how when you tried to read the Bible before you got saved, it seemed confusing, but after you were saved, you were able to understand it with clarity?" When I heard this, I about fell out of my chair. This was exactly my experience, but I previously didn't know why.

You may have the same experience if you try reading the Bible now. I recommend starting with the book of John. Then, continue with the New Testament, starting in Matthew. Read at your own pace and ask God to speak to you as you read. You will understand.

> Ask, and it shall be given you; seek, and ye shall find; knock, and it shall be opened unto you.
> —Matthew 7:7 KJV

Prayer

There are further tests to reveal this new presence of God, the Holy Spirit. Your prayers will be a whole new ballgame. Think of it this way. In the neighborhood where I live, there are many children. I am concerned for their wellbeing, but what I'm willing to do to help them pales in comparison to what I would be willing to do to help my own two children. If you have just trusted Jesus for salvation, you are now a child of God for the first time. God has always loved you, and you were always part of His creation, but now you are one of his own. Remember John 1:12 KJV:

But as many as received him [Jesus], to them gave he power to become the sons of God, even to them that believe on his [Jesus] name:

This means that you have a new, unique access to God, as these next two verses in Ephesians spell out:

So then you are no longer strangers and aliens, but you are fellow citizens with the saints and members of the household of God.... —Ephesians 2:19 ESV

But now in Christ Jesus you who once were far off have been brought near by the blood of Christ.
—Ephesians 2:13 ESV

Now that you have this new unique access put it to use! To pray means to ask. Consider the invitation below:

In that day you will ask nothing of me. Truly, truly, I say to you, whatever you ask of the Father in my name, he will give it to you. 24 Until now you have asked nothing in my name. Ask, and you will receive, that your joy may be full. —John 16:23-24 ESV

There's an important distinction to be made here about prayer. Notice the invocation to pray, "in my name." What this means is we should only ask for those things that God already wants for us. Think of this as asking for those things that are God's will for us.

Sometimes, it's hard to know God's will for us. He certainly wants us to understand the message God has for us in the Bible, so asking God to help you understand the Bible is a prayer that's likely to be answered. Other items can be harder. We know it's God's will for us to be patient, but does He want us to get a promotion or a date with a certain someone? These requests can be less clear. Pray anyway. The Bible says to pray without ceasing.

> Rejoice always, [17] pray without ceasing, [18] give thanks in all circumstances; for this is the will of God in Christ Jesus for you. —1 Thessalonians 5:16-18 ESV

The only way to pray without ceasing is to bring seemingly trivial details to God's attention. That's OK. God is a God of detail. He took an early and detailed interest in you:

> Why, even the hairs of your head are all numbered.... —Luke 12:7 ESV

> Before I formed you in the womb I knew you.... —Jeremiah 1:5 ESV

Therefore, your prayers could include safe travel, thanksgiving for every meal, and so on. Entire books have been written on prayer. The goal is just to get you started—and to put the Spirit of God to the test!

Sin

Now that you are saved, you will have a new sensitivity to sin—both others and your own. This is another test, another manifestation of the Holy Spirit.

You may find foul words that didn't bother you in the past bother you now. You may find forms of entertainment that were pleasurable before just aren't fun anymore. You may lose interest in old friends and gain new Christian friends.

What's happening is a process called sanctification. Sanctification means to be made holy. It's a lifelong process that is never complete. The Holy Spirit will do a work in your life to transform you day by day into the image of Christ. Yet this is not a passive experience—we should be actively seeking after God. What a journey!

Through this process, we want to exercise judgment without being judgmental. Exercising judgement without being judgmental means we take the instructions in scripture as something we can apply to our own lives without worrying about someone else that may seem to be ignoring the instruction.

Consider these verses:

[3] Why do you see the speck that is in your brother's eye, but do not notice the log that is in your own eye? [4] Or how can you say to your brother, 'Let me take the speck out of your eye,' when there is the log in your own eye? [5] You hypocrite, first take the log out of your own eye, and then you will see clearly to take the speck out of your brother's eye.   —Matthew 7:3-5 ESV

The verse above in Matthew is a favorite, but consider this one also:

Why do you pass judgment on your brother? Or you, why do you despise your brother? For we will all stand before the judgment seat of God.

—Romans 14:10 ESV

Let's work though an example that will be, no doubt, very controversial.

I have a friend that I admire. We were friends for a long time before I learned that this friend is gay. The Bible is very clear about homosexual conduct, calling it sin. Therefore, I conclude that I should not engage in homosexual relations. This is easy for me, since I am not at all tempted by same sex attraction. However, not everyone is as blessed as I am. Obviously, homosexuality is something my friend is struggling with, or perhaps no longer struggling, having given in to it.

Does this mean we can no longer be friends? If I can only be friends with the sinless, then I will have no friends.

If my friend asks me whether I think homosexuality is a sin, I'm going to tell him yes—what else could I say? There is one branch of Christianity that needs to be reminded that homosexuality is still a sin and another branch of Christianity that needs to be reminded that Christ died on the cross for the homosexual. Maybe we should stop throwing people out of church for their conduct and instead, throw them back in! Where else can Spirit inspired transformation take place?

Most of us are fortunate to have less visible sin problems, or sin problems that are more acceptable among people. However, nothing is invisible to God and our slipshod lifestyles in our permissive society do not pass muster with God:

> [5] Put to death therefore what is earthly in you: sexual immorality, impurity, passion, evil desire, and covetousness, which is idolatry. [6] *On account of these the wrath of God is coming.* (emphasis mine) [7] In these you too once

walked, when you were living in them. [8] But now you must put them all away: anger, wrath, malice, slander, and obscene talk from your mouth. [9] Do not lie to one another, seeing that you have put off the old self with its practices. —Colossians 3:5–9 (ESV)

Over the years, there have been a couple of occasions when couples have tearfully informed me that their child is gay. I don't mean to make light of their angst and I feel blessed that they felt comfortable sharing their troubles with me. However, aren't they saying their child has a sin problem? And don't we all? How come a parent has never come to me in tears over the fact that their child is a backbiting gossip? Or arrogant and prideful? Are these problems more acceptable?

Consider James 2:10 ESV: For whoever keeps the whole law but fails in one point has become guilty of all of it.

That's a Reality Face Punch! Which sin is it that really boils your blood? Is it murder? How about pedophilia? Drug dealing? Whatever it is, you and I are no better.

One of the greatest Christians of all time was Paul, author of most of the New Testament. He had this to say about himself:

Christ Jesus came into the world to save sinners, of whom I am the foremost. —1 Timothy 1:15 ESV

Let's return to our original premise. Now that you're a Spirit indwelled Christian, your view of sin will never be the same again.

When Things Get Tough

There may be habits of a lifetime that are hard to shake. God may confront us with things that seem impossible. This isn't just a test for us—it's a test of the Holy Spirit.

Indwelling by the same God that created the universe is a powerful attribute! In the end, we live the Christian life the same way we got saved—trusting God to do the work for us that we cannot do. Consider this verse in Romans:

> Likewise, the Spirit helps us in our weakness. For we do not know what to pray for as we ought, but the Spirit himself intercedes for us with groanings too deep for words. —Romans 8:26 (ESV)

What a picture of the Spirit pouring himself out on our behalf even though we didn't know how to ask! And there's more:

> Who is to condemn? Christ Jesus is the one who died— more than that, who was raised—who is at the right hand of God, who indeed is interceding for us. —Romans 8:34 (ESV)

Jesus occupies a favored place with God and is using that high station to intercede for us. That's a power play!

Becoming a New Person

Everything we've been discussing leads to this conclusion. As a result of being saved and by the indwelling power of the Holy Spirit, you may become an entirely different person. I could never have imagined that 25 years ago, I would not only become a follower of Jesus, but I would also want to tell as many as possible about him.

> ...put off your old self, which belongs to your former manner of life and is corrupt through deceitful desires, and to be renewed in the spirit of your minds, and to put on the new self, created after the likeness of God in true righteousness and holiness.
>
> —Ephesians 4:22–24 (ESV)

Contact Me

In the last chapter, I invited you to contact me at saved@davidjdecker.com if reading this book resulted in you being saved. If you contact me, I would also be privileged to pray for any additional needs that you mention. Everything will be kept in complete confidence and never shared with anyone.

Thanks for indulging me on this unusual journey. Sometimes, conversations like these are hard to have. Matthew 5:13 ESV warns of this:

> You are the salt of the earth, but if salt has lost its taste, how shall its saltiness be restored? It is no longer good for anything except to be thrown out and trampled under people's feet.

Salt adds flavor, but it can also be an irritant. It is possible that this message has caused an offense. Even among Christians, it is easy to disagree with nuances of theology. It is never my intention to offend. Therefore, if I have created an offense, let me apologize now.

But understand that it is this message that is the reason for this book. In the greater scheme of things, you may never get to the Super Bowl. But I trust I will see you in Heaven!

If the whole of Christianity were to be summarized into just one sentence, it would be this one: Trust in Jesus Christ alone for your salvation and then tell others about it. If you have already accomplished the first task, you can complete the second by giving others a copy of this book.

God bless you.

Therefore, if anyone is in Christ Jesus, he is a new creation. The old has passed away; behold, the new has come.   —2 Corinthians 5:17 ESV

"

"There are far, far better

things ahead than any we

leave behind."

—C.S. Lewis

"

20

A WORLD WITHOUT LIMITS

The word salary is a Latin term that means money given to soldiers to buy salt or even "salt money." Salt was important in the ancient world because it was used for the preservation of food, religious rituals, and even currency. Perhaps you've heard the cliché, "worth one's salt." This means someone who has earned their place or their pay. For anyone receiving a salary, it could be inferred that they were working to buy salt.

In the US, the average annual per capita consumption of salt is just over seven pounds. Salt seems to come in 26-ounce containers these days, which means you would need five of them to sustain all the salt you would need for a year with a surplus. At a price of $1.79 each, that means the average person in the US consumes about $8.95 per year of salt.

As of this writing, the federally mandated minimum wage is still $7.25. It's hard to imagine that anyone is actually working for so little. It seems like the de facto minimum is much higher, probably $15 per hour. In any case, even the lowest paid worker can earn enough to buy all the salt needed for a year in little more than an hour. Restaurants can deploy saltshakers on a table, knowing that if they get stolen, it would be for the saltshaker, not the salt inside!

In other words, what was once precious is now so cheap it's practically given away. It's a demonstration of a World Without Limits.

We Are Never Going to Run Out of Resources

We are never going to run out of resources. Some might rebel at such a bold claim. How can it be true that on a finite planet composed at the molecular level of a limited number of atoms, we can never run out of them? Human ingenuity is the infinity catalyst.

Human Ingenuity—The Infinity Catalyst

I'm an old school guy. I still like to read a physical newspaper. As a kid, I delivered newspapers. Maybe that's where I got hooked on them.

Back then, newspaper market penetration exceeded 100%. That means the average home was getting more than one newspaper. I still get two of them. A kid like me could walk or ride a bike on a paper route and deliver newspapers to almost every house.

But even when I was young, television and other media sources were beginning to encroach on the newspaper trade. Today, there are no kids delivering newspapers. The houses still getting them are so few and far between that delivery can only be accomplished by automobile. Iconic newspapers like the Detroit Free Press don't even produce a print edition every day anymore. And try finding one of those newspaper boxes you could insert a fist full of change into and get a newspaper. Newspapers aren't even sold in bookstores anymore. Newspapers are about as easy to find as dinosaurs.

The days of cutting down trees and spilling ink to spread the news are quicky coming to an end thanks to the Infinity Catalyst of human ingenuity. Today, news is delivered digitally over the airwaves, internet, or microwave towers. The allocation of atoms to news delivery is trending to zero. Better still, in a world concerned with environmental impact and climate change, the extent of fossil fuels being expended on diesel trucks and gasoline automobiles for news delivery is likewise ending, which is part of why we will also enjoy energy without limits.

Energy Without Limits

Like it or not, the prosperity we enjoy today was achieved by employing cheap and abundant energy. That trend is going to continue into an ever brighter future also run on cheap, abundant energy. But here's a Reality Face Punch for my environmentalist friends. Fossil fuels aren't going anywhere. Renewable energy will supplement, not supplant fossil fuels. The history of this being true is overwhelming.

Different energy forms have always been supplemental. We have yet to see one form of energy replace another. Long ago, wood was a primary energy source. In England, coal mining never supplanted wood. Instead, more wood than ever was consumed along with the coal. In the U.K., there are still wood-burning electric utility plants, and a single one of them uses more wood than Britain's entire 18th-century economy. Yet these wood burning plants only produce a small fraction of current energy output. We are not transitioning to a world fueled by renewable energy. The transition is only to more energy of all kinds.[1]

This will only come as unwelcome news to environmentalists and climate change alarmists. In the meantime, more cheap energy means better hygiene, longer lifespans, and better living conditions for emerging third-world populations. Prosperity also leads to a cleaner environment, for example, by the adoption of natural gas for heating and cooking rather than open fires fueled with wood. It also means more customers and trading partners in an ever more prosperous world.

The Tower of Babel

In the Bible, there is an account in the Book of Genesis Chapter 11 about how a population attempted to build a tower to the heavens. This event includes the message of the gospel because it outlines another attempt by people to reach heaven in their own strength instead of trusting in Jesus. God was not pleased by this tower building and confused the peoples' language, causing them to disperse. The Bible also says there is nothing new under the sun, or that history repeats itself.

We tend to look upon our ancestors with smiling contempt, thinking them to be primitive. But while technology and circumstances change, human nature remains the same. We are equally capable of building our own Towers of Babel, and climate change is certainly one of them. Our ancestors believed they could reach the heavens by building a tower. We think we can change the weather of the planet. Consider this discussion about Jesus in Matthew 8:27 ESV: And the men marveled, saying, "What sort of man is this, that even winds and sea obey him?"

The existential threat facing the world today is not climate change but ambitious authoritarian rulers like those found in Russia, China, Iran, and North Korea. Surprisingly, the latest Russian adventures in Ukraine suggest a future that will see a world at peace.

A World at Peace

Absent worldwide revival, there will always be terrorist attacks, minor skirmishes and conflicts. But full-scale war like the invasion of Ukraine is unlikely to be repeated. There are important lessons in Ukraine for our authoritarian rivals to learn.

Authoritarian police states like China, Russia, Iran, and North Korea need to maintain a cozy relationship with their militaries. The only way they remain in power is by the ability to crush dissent. Lacking a free press to report on corruption and waste, these militaries are not all they seem to be. Nowhere is this more evident than in the Russian invasion of Ukraine. Yet, at least the Russians had some combat experience from actions in Syria and Georgia. The Chinese have not been at war since a bungled invasion of Vietnam in 1979.

The Chinese would like to subject Taiwan to the rule of the Chinese Communist Party, perhaps by invasion if necessary. However, the amphibious invasion of an island like Taiwan is a far more challenging engagement than the disastrous Russian land-born invasion of Ukraine. And should the Chinese attempt such folly, they will expose themselves to be just as incapable as the Russians, if not more so.

There are two possible outcomes for Taiwan: an invasion or no invasion. The probability of invasions seems less in the wake of the Russian experience in Ukraine. However, should the Chinese attack, while no doubt disruptive and tragic, the People's Liberation Army is likely to be neutered in a similar fashion as the Russians. Either the Chinese must remain at peace, or if they become ambitious, the illusion of military prowess will be exposed. The Chinese are better off making threats than acting on them, the more likely outcome. This will be annoying, but the solutions are simple.

The US used to maintain a military base in Taiwan as late as 1979. Strong US leadership could engineer an international coalition of nations to stage a contingent of soldiers on the island such that any sort of attack would immediately envelop many allied countries. No doubt the Chinese would rattle sabers over such a move, and perhaps even attempt a naval blockade of Taiwan. The US and its allies must be prepared to combine their navies to run any blockade. The gambit is peace through strength.

All these military preparations may sound troubling, but the bigger picture and the outcome will be a world at peace.

And a world at peace will enable a technological renaissance to blossom.

> He makes wars cease to the end of the earth …
> —Psalm 46:9 ESV

A Technological Renaissance

Prior to the American Civil War, most US citizens were farmers. As industrialization and urbanization trends emerged, we eventually evolved to the state today where only 1.2% of people are engaged in direct on farm employment (USDA 2022). While the number of workers engaged in farming cratered to almost nothing, the population exploded from 18.5 million in 1865 to about 340 million today. And we are vast exporters of food.

What this describes is an amazing productive accomplishment in agriculture, but it is hardly unique. Today, politicians lament the loss of manufacturing jobs. In the meantime, manufacturing output in the US is holding steady. In other words, manufacturing is experiencing the same outcome as agriculture. We are figuring out how to make things with less labor. Hello again to the Infinity Catalyst of human ingenuity.

And we're just getting started. We've hardly plumbed the depths of the internet and already, artificial intelligence is here. Some experts believe AI will catapult the economy into 30% annual growth rates.[2] I'm skeptical of such ambitious predictions. I think the human capacity to respond to such ongoing and rapid change is limited and will impose a ceiling on such growth. Plus, AI will have uneven adoption. There may be robotic assisted surgeries, but the surgeon is still going to be human. Childcare is still going to be the domain of in person work. Ditto skilled trades and construction. Business management, education, law, media, and sports and fitness are just a few additional areas unlikely to benefit from advances in AI.

Yet, we don't need to see skyrocketing 30% growth rates to experience unprecedented prosperity. Even sustained five to seven percent growth would be double the growth rate of this century and would result in fortunes never experienced in this country.

Longer, Better Lives

Medical miracles are either just on the horizon or already here. New treatments to combat obesity include glucagon-like peptides such as Ozempic. Focused ultrasound waves can target the brain to relieve patients suffering from tremors, including Parkinson's disease. There's further hope that this technology can help with depression, obsessive-compulsive disorders, Alzheimer's, ALS (Lou Gehrig's Disease), and even opioid addiction.

Something called CRISPR gene therapy can repair the genetic mutation responsible for muscular dystrophy. Other treatments hold out hope for a cure for sickle-cell anemia. There are relatively inexpensive blood tests analyzed by AI that look for patterns in blood samples to identify over 50 cancers at the earliest stages. Should cancer be found, early treatment alone already hands the patient a survival advantage. And new treatments are on the horizon.[3]

None of this is new, but only a continuation and perhaps an acceleration of existing trends. Better hygiene, vaccinations, and improved medicines have banished many illnesses that used to kill millions.

A World Without Limits

A recent Pew Research survey measured a growing contingent of parents indicating they were not planning on having children over concerns about the environment and climate change. More childless U.S. adults now say they don't plan to ever have kids.[4]

I'm a little more optimistic.

How tragic to miss out on one of the greatest joys in life over a problem that, if it is a problem, will likely be solved like all our problems, by the Infinity Catalyst of human ingenuity. Perhaps it would have been solved sooner by one of these children if they had them. Declining populations are a greater threat to prosperity than climate change, but even population decline is likely to be solved through the implementation of robotics and automation.

The future holds more opportunity and adventure than we ever imagined.

For I know the plans I have for you," declares the LORD, "plans to prosper you and not to harm you, plans to give you hope and a future.   —Jeremiah 29:11 ESV

ENDNOTES

Chapter 3: The Apollo Solution Part II

1. CNBC, *35% of millionaires say it's 'going to take a miracle' to be ready for retirement, report finds,* Jessica Dickler, 12/2/2022.
2. Tang is a powdered drink mix from General Foods that became popular from its association with the NASA Space program.

Chapter 8: The Secret to Success in Business

1. Sharpsheets, Chick-Fil-A Franchise FDD, Profits & Costs (2025) 06/02/2025
2. Franchise City, *How Much Does A McDonald's Franchise Make?* Article references 2020 sales but is undated with no author.

Chapter 15: The Future of Autonomous Vehicles

1. AAA Foundation for Traffic Safety Research Brief, *American Driving Survey, 2020–2021,* October 2022.

Chapter 16: The Future of Garbage

1. The Guardian, *Internet of bins: smart, solar powered trashcans in Colombian cities,* Elaine Ramirez, 6/14/2016.
   New Atlas, *Bigbelly's Wi-Fi-enabled, solar-powered bins could lead to smarter cities,* 7/21/2015

Chapter 17: A Reality Face Punch Rescue Plan for Young People

1. The Earnest Blog > Paying for College, *Why Is College So Expensive? 6 Reasons (and How to Make it Cheaper),* Carolyn Morris, 3/28/2025.
2. Forbes, *Administrative Bloat At U.S. Colleges Is Skyrocketing,* Paul Weinstein, Jr., 8/28/2023.
3. The Chronicle of Higher Education, *Latest Data: Which Private-College Presidents Earned the Most,* Brian O'Leary and Audrey Williams, 7/24/2023.
1. Boston Magazine – City Life, *How Liberal Professors Are Ruining College,* Chris Sweeney, 12/20/2016
5. Wall Street Journal *Why Americans Have Lost Faith in the Value of College Three generations of 'college for all' in the U.S. has left most families looking for alternatives,* Douglas Belkin, 1/19/2014.

6. St. Louis Post-Dispatch, *On colleges campuses, once a free-thinking safe harbor, oppression now reigns*, Editorial, 3/28/2023
7. CBS News *More than half of college grads are stuck in jobs that don't require degrees,* Megan Cerullo 2/23/2024
8. NPR Education, *High-paying jobs that don't need a college degree? Thousands of them sit empty*, Jon Marcus, 2/14/2023.
9. OnToCollege, *Debt, But No Degree: The College Dropout Crisis,* 9/1/2024

Chapter 20: A World Without Limits

1. Wall Street Journal *Irresistible March of Energy Realism*, Holman W. Jenkins, Jr., 11/20/2024.
2. Vox *How AI could explode the economy – and how it could fizzle* Dylan Matthews, 3/6/2024
3. Wall Street Journal, *Magic Pills are Coming, Wearable ultrasound machines and other inventions could reduce medical costs,* Andy Kessler 11/26/2023
4. Pew Research Center *Growing share of childless adults in U.S. don't expect to ever have children,* Anna Brown 11/19/2021.

www.ingramcontent.com/pod-product-compliance
Lightning Source LLC
Chambersburg PA
CBHW022043210326
41458CB00080B/6639/J